14-35

WAGE DETERMINATION
Market or Power Forces?

Edited with Introductions by
RICHARD PERLMAN
UNIVERSITY OF WISCONSIN — MILWAUKEE

HD 4909
.P45

D. C. HEATH AND COMPANY · BOSTON

CONTENTS

I. THE CONTROVERSY OVER MARGINAL THEORY

Introduction   1

RICHARD A. LESTER
Shortcomings of Marginal Analysis for
Wage-Employment Problems   9

FRITZ MACHLUP
Marginal Analysis and Empirical Research   30

JOHN T. DUNLOP
Productivity and the Wage Structure   55

II. UNION INFLUENCE ON WAGES

Introduction   77

CLARK KERR
Wage Relationships—The Comparative Impact
of Market and Power Forces   80

ROBERT OZANNE

Impact of Unions on Wage Trends and
Income Distribution 104

JOHN E. MAHER

Union, Nonunion Wage Differentials 127

SUGGESTIONS FOR READING 150

INTRODUCTION

Since the mid-1940's, as the mechanics of wage setting have been carried out more and more through collective bargaining, controversy has raged over the issue of the major determinants of wages. The dispute centers about the question of whether market or power forces are more important in determining wages.

Are wages set, within narrow limits, by the inexorable laws of supply and demand, in accordance with marginal productivity theory? Is the bargaining table merely the stage on which these market forces play their parts?

On the other hand, are economic factors merely background elements in the power struggle between labor and management? Are wages determined by the relative bargaining strength of the two groups? Is unionism a new and dominant independent determinant of wages?

The controversy reaches an emotional level in the press and popular literature where the issue is dramatized by the question of whether unions do or do not generate continual, irresistible forces on wages, causing or threatening a variety of economic ills from runaway inflation to our chronic balance of payments deficit. Even the professional literature has reached no definitive response to the question of the relative importance of market and power forces in determining wage levels. Both sides have been able to maintain their positions because the data and studies based on these data have not been conclusive. No single theme, no common factor appears in all wage settings to provide an unequivocal answer to the question of wage determinants.

Both positions have been supported and attacked by logical argument and empirical studies. In general, two broad approaches to the controversy over whether market or power forces determine wages have been used. In one, the economic-forces proponents claim that wages have conformed to marginal productivity theory, and they substantiate their claim with appropriate data. Supported by equally impressive data, the power-forces adherents point out that wages have not conformed to marginal productivity theory.

In the second approach, the former group claims that unionism has not been an important element in wage determination, while the latter group claims that unionism strongly influences wage levels. Again, both positions are well fortified with supporting data.

In this volume, readings have been selected which not only emphasize both sides of the two approaches to the controversy, but which have also stimulated widespread interest because of their novel or pathbreaking nature. The selected works are organized into two sections corresponding to the two approaches. General introductions enumerate many of the statistical and methodological problems which beset studies in this field. The points raised in these introductions have often appeared in the literature, and no claim to originality is made, even if the presentation is somewhat unusual.

Introductions to the selections are designed to acquaint the student with their place in the literature and to summarize their main contributions. Comments at the end of the selections try to relate the main points made to other writings on the particular subject which either support or oppose the methods or conclusions presented. The annotated Bibliography cites sources for the points and issues raised in the Comments, and also provides a guide to the student for further reading among well-known works in the field.

[In the following selections most footnotes, except explanatory ones, have been omitted.]

PART ONE

THE CONTROVERSY OVER MARGINAL THEORY

INTRODUCTION

Part of the difficulty in assigning causative factors in wage determination and concluding whether market or power forces operate, stems from statistical and methodological problems. This study is concerned with these problems insofar as they apply to the marginal productivity theory. Consider the theory's approach to the question of whether economic or bargaining power factors determine wage levels. In its simplest form, under perfect competition, the wage paid to a group of workers equals the value of output attributable to the last (marginal) worker hired.

Statistical Problems

To test whether this equality exists in a given situation involves complex statistical problems. These problems center about the availability of data and the specific meaning of terms in the context of marginal productivity theory.

Availability of Data

In measuring the importance of marginal theory to wage determination, or in appraising the influence of unionism on wages, studies are of course limited by the availability of data. Because of the wealth of manufacturing wage data compiled by the Bureau of Labor Statistics and indirectly by the Census of Manufacturers, most wage studies are of manufacturing industries. Unfortunately, from the point of view of extrapolating the manufacturing experience to other sectors of the economy, the trend of manufacturing employment as a share of total employment has been downward since the late 1940's.

Terms

More serious than data limitation is the elusiveness of the very terms that must be measured to reach conclusions on the determinants of wages. The term "wages" has become increasingly ambiguous today. Labor cost, with its inclusion of fringe benefits, is currently a more meaningful concept than average hourly earnings but is much more difficult to measure.

Furthermore, when speaking of wages, the concept of a labor market must be implied at least in judging the effect of unionism on wages. One would not wish to compare wage changes of male northern, unionized mechanics in the aircraft industry with those of unorganized, unskilled female southern textile laborers. That is to say, the variable of unionism or nonunionism must be isolated from other factors which might lead to differential wages such as differences in occupation, industry, region, or sex; wage comparisons must be made of workers in the same labor market. At the limit, a purist might limit the labor market to workers performing the same job, for the same firm, in the same plant. Obviously, such wage studies would be meaningless. Except for some leeway with job titles and seniority, such workers would receive the same pay and all would or would not be unionized. The decision regarding the effective width of a labor market for wage studies may be a methodological one but it has statistical implications. The wider the market, the more plentiful the data, but the less isolated the union-nonunion variable. The narrower the market, the sharper the union-nonunion dichotomy, but the scantier the data and the less definite the statistical conclusions.

The applicability of marginal theory to wage determination is measured by the closeness to which changes in productivity correspond to changes in wages, in the case of perfect competition in the labor market, and marginal value product in the case of imperfect competition in the labor or product market. In either case, the relevant physical productivity variable is marginal and not average productivity. In practice, it is impossible to measure changes in marginal productivity of labor. Therefore, changes in average productivity must be used as a rough approximation to marginal productivity changes. Furthermore, although changes in output per man-hour are available or can usually be calculated from collected data, these changes often fail to measure the true changes in labor productivity that must be compared with wage movements. Labor is but one of the factors of production to which output changes are attributable. If improvements or additions to capital result in increases in output, it does not follow that the subsequent increase in output per man-hour should result in equivalent wage increases. Although new techniques have been devised to measure changes in output imputable to separate factors, they are difficult to apply to limited studies.

Methodological Problems

Corresponding Wage and Productivity Movement

Returning to the basic tenet of the marginal productivity theory, there is the presumption that, if wages rose without a corresponding increase in value productivity, unemployment would result until productivity rose to the new higher level of wages. Thus, if a statistical study revealed a close correspondence between wage and productivity movements in a given situation in which unions were active in the wage field, it might pose a difficult logical problem to assign the causative element in the wage movement to economic or power forces.

Under the bargaining agreement, management might tend to adjust employment to the bargained wage until marginal value productivity and wages were again equated. If wages were higher than would have been the case had there been no union wage activity and if unemployment had resulted, it would appear that even though wage movements conformed to productivity movements, relative bargaining power was more important than economic forces in determining wages. However, if unemployment resulted because of the higher wage, then though wages were arbitrarily set by power forces, the wage-productivity-employment nexus would have followed a pattern that fitted marginal theory. The addition of the variable unemployment into the scheme of the theory being tested introduces another uncertainty and the analysis becomes more tortuous. If the single question "Do wage movements conform to productivity movements?" is answered affirmatively, then to conclude whether economic forces or relative bargaining strength had greater influence on the wage movement, it is necessary to explore the following questions: (1) Is the established wage higher than would have been set without bargaining? (2) Has the higher wage resulted in unemployment?

If a positive answer is given to both of the latter two questions then it can be concluded that wages, in isolation, were determined by power forces, but that the wage-productivity-employment movements followed marginal theory.

When considering other possible answers to these two questions, it becomes evident that the questions are not independent. If wages were not set higher because of bargaining, then unemployment could not logically be expected to follow.

An involved combination would be for wages to be considered higher than they would have been in a nonbargaining situation, and for no unemployment to have resulted from these higher wages. At first view, this combination of answers would seem to satisfy the power-forces school inasmuch as the wage was determined by relative bargaining strength without resulting in unemployment. But the chief criterion for concluding that an established wage is higher than that which would have prevailed under free market conditions is the presence of unemployment. Without this unemployment, the higher wages must have conformed to marginal theory, in the absence of significant changes in physical productivity, by being accompanied by equivalently higher product prices. Thus, the conclusion of whether market or power forces determined wages would be transformed into the question of whether the higher prices caused, or were caused by, higher wages. In the former case, wage movements would have resulted from market forces—bargaining holding up real wages; in the latter case from power forces—wages being the independent variable in the wage-price-productivity system.

Thus, with the absence of unemployment as a guide, as would be the case in a growing prosperous situation, the decision of whether market or power forces determined wages would hinge on the presence of "cost-push" or "demand-pull" inflation. Economists have been wrangling for years over just this crucial point of which came first, higher prices or higher wages, and have not yet reached conclusions nor criteria definite enough to be applied to the theory of wage determination.

The final combination of responses of wages and unemployment to the condition of corresponding wages and value productivity movements would be for wages under bargaining to rise no higher than they would have without bargaining, with, of course, no effect on the level of employment. At first view, this set of conditions would seem to describe an ideal case of the operation of market forces—wages moving in strict accordance with productivity theory unaffected by relative power forces. However, because the overall, or resultant, force on wages of power forces is zero, it does not signify that the power struggle between labor and management did not operate in the wage area. A zero resultant may represent the combined force of two opposite forces; that is, if management and labor shared equal strength at the bargaining table, the bargained wage might approach the same level as indicated by market forces alone. Thus, the condition of corresponding wage and value productivity changes at "market forces" level of wages might reflect either the absence of significant power forces or the neutralization of conflicting power forces.

The following outline of conditions and conclusions summarizes the various evaluations, reached above, concerning the relative importance of market and power forces.

Corresponding Wage and Productivity Changes

I. Bargained wage above level if no bargaining.
   (a) Unemployment.
      Conclusion: Power forces determine wages.
   (b) No unemployment.
      1. Higher wages lead to higher prices.
         Conclusion: Power forces determine wages.
      2. Higher prices lead to higher wages.
         Conclusion: Market forces determine wages (though bargaining power is evident to protect real wages from effects of inflation).

II. Bargained wage no higher than if no bargaining.
   Conclusion: Market forces determine wages.

or

Equal and opposite power forces determine wages.

Divergent Wage and Value Productivity Movements

If wage movements do not conform to value productivity changes, then obviously wages do not accord with marginal theory. But this evidence against the marginalists does not at the same time provide positive support for the power-forces school. A variety of reasons, other than the relative bargaining power exercised by unions and management, can explain the divergence of wage and productivity changes.

If workers are paid less than their marginal value product, it might indicate they are in a weak bargaining position. Under competitive conditions in the labor market, behaving like true marginalists they would move to higher paying jobs. But studies indicate that the typical worker is not quite the "economic man" adherence to marginalism requires him to be. He might consider pleasant working conditions, resistance to change, or seniority benefits as sufficient reasons for submitting to economic exploitation—accepting a wage below his marginal value product. If he does so under a nonunion setting, it signifies that marginalism does not apply. To stretch a point, it might be conceded that he has a weak bargaining position with regard to wages because of his interest in nonwage matters.

Now, if he accepts an "exploitative" wage under collective bargaining, it again indicates that marginalism does not apply. It might again reflect the same weak bargaining position with regard to wages as in the nonunion setting because of his interest in nonwage matters, or, instead, it might reflect the weaker bargaining position of the union vis-à-vis management. But the mere presence of a depressed wage in a union setting does not necessarily signify that the lower wage resulted from lack of union strength. More relevantly, it need not signify that there was something inherent in the setting of the wage through bargaining rather than by its arbitrary setting by management, as would have been the case in a nonbargaining situation, that led to a wage lower than the level corresponding to the marginal value product of the (unionized) work force.

Just as great uncertainty arises in judging the relative merits of the productivity and power schools when the bargained wage is higher than the level of the marginal value product. Again, marginal theory maintains both that workers would be laid off until marginal value product rose to the higher wage and that while this is done firms are making less than maximum profits. Again, this condition might reflect bargaining weakness in one of the wage negotiators—this time, management. But again it might reflect this weakness not because of anything inherent in the bargaining process itself, that is, in the power struggle between unions and management.

Management might have goals other than profit maximization, such as the reduction of labor turnover, the strengthening of worker morale, or in the case of firms operating under conditions of monopolistic competition, discouragement of government intervention and regulation, or improvement in public relations by acquiring the reputation of being generous employers. Then, too, during prosperous periods when profits are higher, management might not feel compelled to play the role of the marginalist's economic man, struggling for the last penny of profits. All of these reasons could explain the prevalence of a wage above the value productivity level in either a union or nonunion wage setting.

Selected Papers

A collection of papers which purport to treat the subject of the applicability of marginal analysis to actual wage setting must include Lester's "Shortcomings of Marginal Analysis for Wage-Employment Problems." In a field such as wage determination, where the literature is so compendious, a reviewer runs a risk of error when he claims any single work was the first to introduce a particular theme. Yet, if Lester was not the first to test the applicability of marginalism empirically, his paper has certainly come to be accepted as a reference point for further studies of this issue.

Lester's research led him to the conclusion that wage determination was little influenced by marginal considerations. It cannot be contended by the power-forces school that Lester's denial of marginalism as an important factor led him to accept the relative strength of unions and management as the prime determinant of wage levels. Lester still concluded that economic elements were important in determining wage levels, but that marginal considerations themselves were unimportant. Power-school advocates were quick to note that if the smooth working of marginal theory did not apply, the remaining disjointed economic elements were all subject to power influences.

The doctrine of marginalism, which enjoyed wide acceptance

for a hundred years, was not without its defenders from Lester's empirical attack. The opposition to antimarginalism is best summarized by including portions of Machlup's well-known critique, "Marginal Analysis and Empirical Research." (Space limitations prevent presentation of the entire article.) Machlup, in his attempt to restore marginalism's prestige, questions both Lester's methods and his conclusions. Machlup's reconstruction of marginalism is based on logical arguments, not empirical research.

While Lester tested the influences of marginalism directly by inquiring whether firms behaved as if they adhered to marginal considerations in their wage-employment practices, Dunlop tested it indirectly by a statistical study of whether actual wage experience followed marginal principles. His "Productivity and the Wage Structure," the last selection in this section on marginalism, is a statistical study of the relationship of industrial wage and productivity movements. Although earlier studies compared changes in these variables, Dunlop was the first to conclude that wages moved more or less in accordance with marginal principles. Perhaps Dunlop's paper would not have caused such a stir had he not concluded that "this theoretical framework for interindustry wage movement appears to give no distinctive place to the role of labor organizations." Of course, this remark set off opposing statistical studies which showed that unionism was influential in wage setting. These are discussed in the second section, "Union Influences on Wages." Other studies of the interaction of marginalism and wage movements followed Dunlop's and often gave a weak role to marginalism. These are not included but merely summarized along with an appraisal of Dunlop's approach, because in the main they follow Dunlop's statistical procedures.

RICHARD A. LESTER

Shortcomings of Marginal Analysis
for Wage-Employment Problems*

Dissatisfied with the inconclusive state of the theoretical view of the importance of marginal principles in business decisions on wages and employment, Lester conducted an empirical study of the issue. By use of the questionnaire method, he asked a representative number of southern firms questions designed to find out whether they followed marginal analysis in their wage employment policies. The responses, Lester concluded, were overwhelmingly in the negative. The firms generally replied that they would not reduce employment if wages rose, and that in any case, they did not even use marginal calculations in their employment decisions.

Lester's contention that the evidence of his study indicated that marginal theory was unimportant in business decisions was soon challenged. Machlup's paper (only the parts that refer to Lester's study are included here) presents the marginalist view.

THE conventional explanation of the output and employment policies of individual firms runs in terms of maximizing profits by equating marginal revenue and marginal cost. Student protests that their entrepreneurial parents claim not to operate on the marginal principle have apparently failed to shake the confidence of the textbook writers in the validity of the marginal analysis. Indeed, the trend over the past decade has been to devote more space in elementary textbooks to complicated graphs illustrating marginal relationships and to detailed discussions of marginal analysis under a variety of assumed circumstances.

A gap, however, exists between marginal theory of the firm and

* Reprinted by permission of the author from the *American Economic Review*, XXXVI (March 1946), pp. 63–82.

general theories concerning employment, money, and the business cycle. Textbooks that spend so much of the students' time on the mathematics of profit maximization according to marginal analysis may not mention that principle at all in chapters dealing with the price level, the business cycle, national income, etc. The respective rôles of markets and costs in determining output and employment are not clearly explained. The hiatus exists in Keynes's *General Theory*, despite his efforts to avoid inhabiting two separate theoretical worlds. He fails to reconcile his continued adherence to the marginal-productivity theory with his new theories of employment determination, based on effective demand.

This paper does not pretend to bridge the gap between individual-firm theory and general theory. In examining the relationship between wages and employment from the point of view of the individual firm and investigating the shortcomings of marginal analysis for wage-employment matters, it does, however, represent a step in that direction. Much more evidence must be accumulated before definitive conclusions can be drawn regarding wage-employment relationships. The tentative conclusions of this paper are based on scattered evidence, including new material collected by the author, partly from discussions with numerous Southern business executives but mainly in the form of written replies by 50-odd concerns to questions concerning the relative rôle of different factors in determining their employment, alterations in their variable costs per unit with changes in rate of output, and their probable adjustments to an increase in wages relative to those paid by competing producers.[1]

As much of the evidence in the paper rests on the written replies of 58 Southern concerns, a brief explanation of the selection and collection procedures used is given at this point. A detailed questionnaire was mailed in June, 1945, to the presidents or executive officers of 430 Southern manufacturing firms in industries known to have a significant North-South wage differential. Anonymous reply was possible and most answers were not identified. A total of 68 replies were received. However, 10 firms answered that most of the questions were too difficult or would require too much time to answer, so that only 58 of the replies contain answers to two or more of the questions. The 58 replies are distributed as follows by industry: 17 furniture producers, 13 metal-working firms (foundry, machinery and valve producers), 11 cotton clothing manufacturers (producing

---

[1] Financial support for this study has been supplied by the General Education Board.

work clothes, men's shirts, women's dresses, and cotton underwear), 4 full-fashioned hosiery manufacturers, 3 producers of shoes and leather, 3 paint producers, 4 chemical manufacturers, and 3 stove producers.[2] Employment in these 58 firms averaged 600 (range 8[3] to 8,200).

I

The relative importance of various factors (market demand, wage rates, non-labor costs, profits, production techniques, etc.) in determining the volume of employment offered by a firm constituted the subject matter of the first set of questions in the questionnaire. The objective was to obtain the judgment or opinion of the business executives, partly because policy decisions in those firms presumably are based largely upon such opinions.

The executives were asked: "What factors have generally been the most important ones in determining the volume of employment in your firm during peacetime?" They were requested to rate the factors in terms of the percentage of importance of each; the total was not to exceed a rating of 100 per cent, and, if one factor alone was important, it was to be marked 100 per cent. The listing of the factors was as follows:

a. Present and prospective market demands (sales) for your products, including seasonal fluctuations in demand.
b. The level of wage rates or changes in the level of wages.
c. The level of material costs and other non-wage costs and changes in the level of such non-labor costs.
d. Variations in profits or losses of the firm.
e. New techniques, equipment, and production methods.
f. Other factors (please specify).

The answers gave overwhelming emphasis to current and prospective market demand for products of the firm as the important factor in determining its volume of employment. Out of 56 usable replies, 28 (or one-half) rated factor *a* (market demand) at 100 per cent. Both shoe producers, 3 out of the 4 full-fashioned hosiery firms,

---

[2] The 430 companies to which questionnaires were sent were distributed as follows: 103 furniture, 59 metal-working, 146 cotton clothing, 23 full-fashioned hosiery, 19 shoes and leather, 25 paint and varnish, 17 chemicals, and 30 stoves. Only companies located entirely in the South were selected, and practically all of them were located in only one community. Geographically the replying firms are confined to the following states: Alabama, Arkansas, Florida, Georgia, Louisiana, North Carolina, Tennessee, Texas, and Virginia.

[3] The next smallest firms are two with 25 employees each.

and 11 out of the 16 furniture manufacturers were in that category; on the other hand, only 3 out of the 11 cotton clothing concerns and none of the 3 paint companies rated market demand 100 per cent.

The replies of the other 28 firms that rated two or more factors as important are summarized in Table I.

Factor *b* (wages and changes in wage levels) and factor *d* (profits) are rated surprisingly low by the executive officers of these 56 firms in view of the emphasis placed on those two factors by marginal analysis. On the other hand, the relative stress placed on materials and other non-labor costs as a factor in determining the

TABLE I — RELATIVE IMPORTANCE OF FACTORS INFLUENCING A FIRM'S EMPLOYMENT AS INDICATED BY WEIGHTING GIVEN BY 28 FIRMS RATING 2 OR MORE FACTORS

	a (Market)	b (Wages)	c (Non-labor costs)	d (Profits)	e (Technique)	f (Others)
Number of times mentioned	28	13	18	11	16	5
Average weight per time mentioned	65%	15%	14%	13%	17%	16%
Average for all 28 replies	65.0%	7.6%	9.5%	5.1%	9.7%	3.1%

firm's volume of employment is surprisingly high. Non-labor costs are mentioned more frequently than wages, and they are considered more important than wages in determining the volume of employment by the replying firms in the furniture, cotton clothing, paint, and chemical industries. Indeed, wages are not given a rating at all by any of the replying paint or chemical concerns, and only one out of 6 metal-working firms marking two or more factors gave any weight to wage item *b*. Yet labor costs were an important element in the total costs of practically all of these firms.[4]

[4] Each firm was requested to state the percentage that labor costs are of its total costs. The average for all replying firms was labor costs 29.3 per cent of total costs (range 12 to 60 per cent). The average was 23 per cent for shoes and leather, 24 per cent for paint, 25 per cent for furniture, 31 per cent for chemicals, 33 per cent for cotton clothing, full-fashioned hosiery, and stoves, and 39 per cent for metal-working concerns. Judging by census data, the average for all manufacturing is around 20 per cent.

The relative rating of item *e* (new techniques and changes in production methods) is not unexpected. The other factors mentioned under item *f* included "competition" and "management," which might perhaps have been properly included under items *a* and *e*. Replies of at least two firms indicated a realization that the various factors listed were not completely independent. That was, of course, correct.[5]

The failure to lay more stress on wages as a factor in determining the volume of employment is all the more surprising in view of the relatively high ratio of labor to total cost in most of the replying firms. Indeed, the correlation is remarkably low between the stress placed on wages as an employment factor and the percentage that labor costs are of the firm's total costs. True, 5 out of the 11 concerns with labor costs constituting from 40 to 60 per cent of total costs marked wages as an important item in determining the firm's employment,[6] whereas only one of the 10 firms with wages from 12 to 20 per cent of total costs did so. However, only one-tenth of the firms with wages ranging from 30 to 39 per cent of the total cost mentioned wages as an important employment factor, whereas one-third of the firms with labor costs ranging from 21 to 29 per cent of total costs marked wages along with one or more other factors.

In qualifying or elaborating their answers regarding the rôle of present and prospective demand for the firm's product, 8 concerns explained that they manufacture for stock during dull seasons, 3 others said that demand for their products had been stable or steadily increasing before the war, and 2 others replied that the operation of their equipment requires "just so many men," so that "during peacetime employment is more or less permanent."

It is clear from numerous interviews that most business executives do not think of employment as a function of wage rates but as a function of output.[7] When questioned regarding the employment effects of increased or reduced wages they usually end up by stating that orders, not wage changes, are the important factor in output and

[5] For example, wages affect profits and may influence the introduction of new techniques.

[6] The top firm, with labor costs at 60 per cent of total cost, was not, however, one of the 5.

[7] That our business men are no different in this regard from business men abroad seems to be indicated by experience in Germany under the "Papen Plan" for economic recovery introduced in September, 1932. Through tax subsidies and other concessions, German entrepreneurs were able to hire additional workers, on the average, for about half the existing wage rates. Although

employment. As explained in Section III below, business executives generally do not think of deliberate curtailment of operations and employment as an adjustment to wage increases, partly because some plants and operations require fixed crews under existing techniques of production and partly because, as indicated under Section II below, business men believe the variable costs per unit of production increase as production and employment are curtailed.

II

In recent years a number of attempts have been made to discover the way costs vary with changes in output. Individual-firm studies by Joel Dean and Theodore O. Yntema indicate that average variable costs (and marginal costs) tend to be constant per unit of product over the usual range of output, which includes up to practically full capacity. Other statistical studies suggest that a great number of American manufacturing firms operate under increasing average variable labor returns, primarily because marginal labor requirements decrease per unit as output rises toward full capacity. Some studies indicate a definite tendency, especially in the durable goods industries, toward decreasing marginal cost of production, at least until almost full capacity is reached.

In the present study, a series of questions was asked regarding unit variable costs and profits at various rates of output. In reply to the question, "At what level of operations are your profits generally greatest under peacetime conditions?" 42 firms answered 100 per cent of plant capacity. The remaining 11 replies ranged from 75 to 95 per cent of capacity.[8] Six of the 11 did not answer succeeding questions that would have supplied substantiating data. Some of them said these succeeding questions were "too theoretical" or "too technical," or that "data were not available for an exact answer." One simply stated: "Our cost is based on 90 per cent of capacity." Of the 5 firms that did offer substantiating material, 3 gave cost estimates and 2

such wage reduction for additional employees might have been expected to increase employment, employers hesitated to increase employment and output without an increase in orders, so that unemployment in Germany increased about 20 per cent during the 5 months following introduction of the plan. See Gerhard Colm, "Why the 'Papen Plan' for Economic Recovery Failed," *Social Research*, Vol. I (Feb., 1934), especially pp. 90–91.

See also E. Ronald Walker's opinion based on Australia's experience during the 1930's in *From Economic Theory to Policy* (Chicago, Univ. of Chicago Press, 1943), pp. 73–74.

[8] These 11 firms were distributed as follows: 1 in furniture, 3 in cotton clothing, 2 in paint, 1 in chemicals, 1 in stoves, and 3 in metal-working.

gave the following reasons: "Assuming that if we were at 100 per cent we would have to pay considerable overtime wages," and "Theoretical 100 per cent is likely to produce too many strains."

The executives were also asked how, in peacetime, their factory operating costs (excluding overhead or fixed charges) per unit of output are usually affected by an increase or a decrease in the company's rate of operations. More specifically they were asked the percentage by which an increase in operations from 95 to 100 per cent (also 90 to 95 per cent, 80 to 90 per cent, and 70 to 80 per cent) would tend to result in a rise or fall in operating or variable costs per unit of output. The answers are summarized in Table II for 32 firms giving data indicating they have decreasing marginal variable costs up to 100 per cent capacity,[9] along with 3 firms giving data showing increasing marginal costs beginning at 90, 80, and 75 per cent of capacity.[10] Firms reporting decreasing unit costs up to 100 per cent of capacity have also been classified according to the percentage that their labor costs are of total costs, and averages for 4 categories of labor-cost ratios are given.

The following table indicates some differences in the slope of the average decreasing unit cost curve for different industries. The decline is especially sharp for the metal-working firms and for others (full-fashioned hosiery, shoes, and chemicals) at operations between 70 and 90 per cent of plant capacity. For furniture firms, on the other hand, the rate of decrease in unit variable costs is reported to be higher from 95 to 100 per cent or from 90 to 95 per cent of capacity than it is from 70 to 80 per cent or 80 to 90 per cent of capacity.

The answers seem to indicate that the percentage of labor to total cost of production has little direct influence upon the slope of the decreasing unit cost curve at operations between 70 and 100 per cent

[9] An additional firm stated that its variable costs per unit decreased with increased operations from 70 to 100 per cent of capacity but it did not offer any percentage figures.

A study by the Oxford economists indicated that 13 firms were operating under conditions of decreasing costs, 4 under conditions of constant cost, and 2 under increasing costs. See R. L. Hall and C. J. Hitch, "Price Theory and Business Behaviour," *Oxford Economic Papers,* No. 2 (May, 1939), p. 20, footnote 1.

[10] A total of 17 firms that answered the other questions declined to attempt answers to this one, giving such reasons as "don't know," "no accurate figures," "no exact answers," and "too much theory." In addition, 4 firms gave non-numerical answers that roughly indicated the character of their cost-output relations; their answers are referred to in the text.

TABLE II — DECLINE IN UNIT VARIABLE COST WITH INCREASE IN SCALE
OF OUTPUT

	Increase of operations (in % of plant capacity)			
	95 to 100%	90 to 95%	80 to 90%	70 to 80%
Average for 33 firms with maximum profits at 100% capacity	5.5%	5.7%	7.7%	9.5%
14 furniture firms	6.4	5.9	4.6	5.2
7 cotton-clothing firms	5.6	4.9	6.9	7.5
6 metal-working firms	4.8	7.9	12.5	15.9
6 others	4.7	5.4	9.6	13.9
Average for decreasing cost firms with labor-to-total-cost ratios from				
40 to 60% (6 firms)	4.1%	4.4%	6.6%	8.1%
30 to 39% (6 firms)	2.1	2.3	4.3	5.2
21 to 29% (13 firms)	8.1	7.2	5.8	5.5
12 to 20% (6 firms)	1.9	2.0	4.2	6.2
3 firms with maximum profits at 90, 80, and 75% of capacity				
1 cotton-clothing firm	1.0% rise	1.0% drop	1.5% drop	4.0% drop
1 paint producer	25.0% rise	25.0% rise	10.0% rise	0.0%
1 chemical concern	10.0% rise	? rise	? rise	0.0%

of capacity. The average slope of the unit cost curve for firms with labor-cost ratios from 40 to 60 per cent resembles that of the curve for firms with ratios from 12 to 20 per cent. The peculiar slope of the average curve for firms with labor-cost ratios from 21 to 29 per cent apparently is largely explained by the fact that furniture firms predominate, representing 9 of the 13 firms in that classification.

Constant unit variable costs between the range of 70 and 100-per cent capacity operations were reported by 3 firms.[11] In addition, 2 concerns[12] reported such constant costs between 90 and 100 per cent of capacity, and 6 others[13] gave figures showing a per unit cost variation of no more than from 1 to 8 per cent over the whole range from 70 to 100 per cent of capacity. The president of one chemical firm,

[11] Two in furniture and one in clothing. To quote from the explanation of two of them: "Our unit cost remains the same if you exclude overhead and fixed charges," and "As long as overhead and fixed charges are excluded, the unit cost would not vary much either way, if any."

[12] One in furniture and one in metal-working.

[13] Three in furniture, two in shoes, and one in metal-working.

not included in the above data, replied: "I am not in a position to estimate exact answers, but believe that operating costs in the brackets you outline would vary little. Of course, costs would fall if we increased our operations from 70 to 100 per cent."

As further checks on the replies of the executives, they were asked: "Under normal peacetime conditions, is it possible at times to reduce your operating costs per unit of output by lowering your rate of operations?" Of 44 replies, 43 were "no" and one was "yes." Some replying "no" qualified their answers. One said, "By reducing from more than 100% of capacity to 100%, costs are likely to fall." Another added, "If we work regular hours 100% capacity is point of greatest efficiency and lowest cost but may not be if that involves a great deal of overtime." A number remarked that plant efficiency tends to fall as operations are reduced, that payroll costs do not increase in direct proportion to the volume of operations so that operating costs per unit are lower at higher levels of output, or that operating costs per unit always are lower as 100-per-cent capacity production is approached. The firm answering "yes" gave as its explanation of how lowered operations would permit lower unit variable costs: "Get rid of all incompetent employees, cease selling to chiselers and risky accounts, do more of work instead of paying some one else to do it."

A few of the answers to this question raise doubts as to the validity of the replies of some firms to previous cost questions, particularly those reporting increasing marginal variable costs beginning at 75 to 95 per cent of capacity. Two of the replies may also indicate a failure to distinguish clearly between fixed and variable costs. Nine of the firms reporting maximum profits at 75 to 95 per cent of capacity answered "no" to this question as to whether it was possible to reduce unit variable costs by lowering the rate of operations.[14] Those 9 included the 3 firms that reported U-shaped cost curves, with rising unit variable costs beginning at 75, 80, and 90 per cent of capacity. Two of them were the only replying firms in their industries that reported such cost curves below 100 per cent of capacity.[15]

The significant conclusion from the data in this section is that most of the manufacturing firms in the industries covered by this survey apparently have decreasing unit variable costs within the

[14] The other two of the 11 firms in that category failed to answer this question.

[15] Seven other cotton-clothing firms and 3 other chemical concerns definitely reported decreasing unit costs. The other paint companies gave no detailed cost figures. One reported maximum profits at 100 per cent of capacity and the other at 80 per cent of capacity.

range of 70 to 100 per cent of capacity production — or at least their executive officials believe that to be the case, which is the important factor in determining company policy, whatever the actual facts may be.[16]

If company output and employment policies are based on the assumption of decreasing marginal variable cost up to full capacity operations, much of the economic reasoning on company employment adjustments to increases or decreases in wage rates is invalid, and a new theory of wage-employment relationships for the individual firm must be developed.

The Oxford economists found that a great majority of the business entrepreneurs they questioned[17] "were in profound ignorance" regarding the elasticity of demand for their products and that "answers to questions about increasing or decreasing marginal prime costs were seldom given with confidence."[18] Their sample "erred, if at all, by being biased in favor of well-organized and efficiently conducted businesses," and the entrepreneurs convinced the economists that uncertainty concerning elasticities of demand and marginal prime cost were "due not to any negligence or lack of zeal for knowledge" on the part of the business men "but to the nature of the case."[19] The economists concluded that the results of their study "seem to vitiate any attempts to analyse normal entrepreneurial behaviour in the short period in terms of marginal curves. They also make it impossible to assume that wages in the short run will bear any close relation to the marginal product (or marginal revenue) of the labour employed."[20]

The present author's interviews with business men indicate that most entrepreneurs do not tend to think in terms of marginal variable cost. The heads of manufacturing concerns hiring, say, 50 or more

[16] The T.N.E.C. study of *Industrial Wage Rates, Labor Costs and Price Policies* (monog. no. 5, 1940) revealed that unit labor costs increased as volume fell and declined as rate of operations expanded in the International Harvester Company's plants and in the plants of two paper companies; operating efficiency was lower when volume was small, partly because of more frequent shifting with shorter runs (see pp. xix, xx, 35–37, and 117–19).

[17] Apparently the statements quoted in this paragraph rest primarily on the evidence of 38 of the entrepreneurs interviewed.

[18] R. F. Harrod, "Price and Cost in Entrepreneurs' Policy," *Oxford Economic Papers*, No. 2 (May, 1939), pp. 4, 5.

[19] *Ibid.*, p. 5.

[20] R. L. Hall and C. J. Hitch, "Price Theory and Business Behaviour," *Oxford Economic Papers*, No. 2, p. 32.

workers consider such a procedure both unnecessary and impractical because (1) they seem convinced that their profits increase as the rate of operations rises, at least until full plant capacity is reached — they have no faith in the validity of U-shaped marginal variable cost curves unless, perhaps, overtime pay is involved; (2) they consider repeated shifts in the size of a plant's working force, or in its equipment, with changes in the relative costs of different productive factors to be impractical, their adjustments to cost changes taking most frequently the form of product shifts that require little, if any, alteration in equipment; and (3) they see the extreme difficulty of calculating marginal variable costs and the marginal productivity of factors, especially in multiprocess industries and under present accounting methods. In thinking about employment in their firm, therefore, they tend to emphasize current and prospective demand for their products and the full-crew requirements for their existing facilities, rather than the current level of wage rates.

III

The practical and technical difficulties involved in attempting to apply the marginal analysis to wage-employment matters deserve more attention than can be given them here. This discussion only indicates some of the problems involved in shifting the proportion of factors in manufacturing plants or in calculating the marginal contributions of factors, and, at the same time, points to certain disturbing data.

There is a lack of good case material on the redistribution of factors purely in response to increases or decreases in wage rates. The very existence of unused plant capacity indicates that it is not feasible to substitute capital equipment for labor; otherwise that would have been done because the use of such idle equipment is practically "costless" in view of the fact that fixed charges on it cannot be avoided.

Most industrial plants are designed and equipped for a certain output, requiring a certain work force. Often effective operation of the plant involves a work force of a given size.[21] Certain techniques of production, allowing little variation in the use of labor, may be the only practical means of manufacturing the product.

[21] That, for example, is largely true of automatic-machine tending (such as is characteristic of pulp and paper plants, metal and oil refineries, chemical plants, textile mills, etc.) and of assembly-line operations. It is also true that the size of the work force is largely fixed in service lines like banks, rail and bus transportation, theaters, postal delivery, etc.

Under such circumstances, management does not and cannot think in terms of adding or subtracting increments of labor except perhaps when it is a question of expanding the plant and equipment, changing the equipment, or redesigning the plant. The flexibility of many plants is, however, extremely limited, especially those designed for early stages of manufacturing, such as the smelting, refining, compounding, and rolling of materials.

From much of the literature the reader receives the impression that methods of manufacture readily adjust to changes in the relative costs of productive factors. But the decision to shift a manufacturing plant to a method of production requiring less or more labor per unit of output because of a variation in wages is not one that the management would make frequently or lightly. Such action involves the sale (at a loss?) of existing facilities not usable under the new method and the purchase of new facilities and equipment to replace those discarded, to say nothing of retraining workers and readapting the whole organization.[22] Such new investment presumably would not be undertaken simply to reduce a current and expected net loss, or if there was a likelihood that the wage change would only be temporary or that the cost relationships between factors would be considerably altered again in the near future.[23]

Those who argue for wage reductions on the grounds that a certain relationship exists between wage rates and employment tend to overlook the fact that a shift to less capitalistic or more labor-consuming method may be impractical not only for reasons given above but also because the skilled workers necessary to operate the antiquated equipment are no longer available. Indeed, as Randall Hinshaw points out, writers who believe a wage reduction will tend to stimulate new investment often appear to assume that the investment will be in the form of the most up-to-date equipment, which would require less rather than more labor per unit of output. That, of course, would be contrary to what one might expect from marginal analysis.

That industry does not adapt its plants and processes to varying wage rates in the manner assumed by marginalists seems to be indi-

---

[22] Not to mention countless other problems like the effect of any lay-offs on the company's unemployment tax under experience rating, possible changes in its property-tax assessment, or resulting changes in employee or community attitudes.

[23] The management might also hesitate to take such action if the market value of facilities and equipment to be sold was expected to rise, or if the market value of the equipment to be bought was expected to fall, or if marked improvements in technique were in the offing.

cated by data recently collected by the author. Executives of 112 firms with plants in both the North and the South were asked in January, 1945, the following question: "Have lower wages in the South *themselves* caused your company to use production techniques or methods in its Southern plant(s) that require more labor and less machinery than the proportions of labor to machinery used in its Northern plant(s)?" Of 44 replies, one was vaguely affirmative, one was indefinite, and 42 answered "no." Of the 42, a total of 35 stated that, for all comparable jobs, average wages in their Southern plants were below the average for their Northern plants. On that basis, the wages in the Southern plants averaged per firm from 5 to 30 per cent below the Northern plants, with the average North-South differential for all 35 firms at 15 per cent. Those 35 replying firms represent a wide variety of industries[24] and had a total of over half a million employees in 150 plants in the South and 491 plants in the North. Some of them stated that the existence of lower wages in the South did not influence the type of machinery installed nor the processes used there, that "the most efficient equipment available" is used in every plant regardless of location or relative wage levels.

The sample probably contains offsetting biases: in favor of concerns in a good position to make close comparative cost calculations and in favor of large firms with relatively low labor-to-total-cost ratios. Nevertheless, it should be pointed out that included in the 35 concerns are 15 in industries that, on the average, have labor costs amounting to 25 to 40 per cent of total production costs[25] and 11 that were paying wage rates in the South from 20 to 30 per cent below their comparable Northern rates. Surely, if wage rates were as important in determining the proportion of factors of a firm's employment as the textbooks imply, the completely negative results from this test would not have been possible.

A T.N.E.C. study of wage rates, labor costs, and technological change in two shoe companies, two paper companies, two mills of a textile company, and plants of the International Harvester Company in the 1930's indicated that increases in wage rates were not the most important or decisive factor — in fact may have no significant influence — in the determination and timing of technological changes.

[24] Including 7 cotton and rayon textile firms, 5 building materials producers, 4 food companies, 3 rubber companies, and 2 firms in each of the following industries: clothing, hosiery, oil, chemicals, paper and pulp, metals, furniture and plywood, and aircraft and construction equipment.

[25] Cotton textiles, full-fashioned hosiery, furniture, cotton clothing, and rubber.

For the most part there appeared to be little causal connection between increased labor costs and the introduction of capital improvements.

There is no need to discuss at length in this paper the technical difficulties involved in any attempt to discover the marginal product of an added unit of labor in large-scale industry and to impute to that unit of labor its value contribution to a joint, multi-processed product. Such difficulties have been discussed elsewhere in detail by the author. More recently W. J. Eiteman has succinctly explained the "hopeless complexity" that would attend any attempt to apply marginal analysis to modern manufacturing establishments. His demonstration leaves no doubt that it would be utterly impractical under present conditions for the manager of a multi-process plant[26] to attempt, by means of repeated variation in the number of men employed, to work out and equate marginal costs and marginal returns for each productive factor.

IV

The foregoing discussion and data throw light on experience under the Fair Labor Standards act that has been difficult to explain by conventional marginal theory, and they also help to illuminate the answers of Southern business executives to a group of questions on probable adjustments to an increase in their wage rates relative to those paid by competitors in other regions.

For example, the South-North wage differential in the men's cotton garment industry (shirts, collars, nightwear, work clothes, and pants) was reduced, on the average, by one-third between March, 1939, and March, 1941, primarily as a result of the establishment of a statutory minimum of 30 cents in October, 1939, under the Fair Labor Standards act and an industry wage order setting minimum wages in the industry at 32½ to 40 cents (depending on the product), effective in July, 1940; yet between March, 1939, and March, 1941, employment in 180 identical plants increased more than one and a half times as fast in the South as in the North.[27]

The same pressure of minimum wages had similar results in the wood furniture industry. Between October, 1937, and February, 1941, the South-North wage differential was reduced about 7 per cent for 72 identical wood furniture plants, with the establishment

[26] A plant in which more than one type of operation or process is performed and which has, therefore, more than one "cost center."

[27] Separate figures for branches of the industry show somewhat varying results. Employment did decrease slightly in Southern plants producing shirts, collars, and nightwear, where the North-South wage differential was being

of a statutory minimum of 25 cents in October, 1938, and 30 cents in October, 1939, and the setting of minima from 32½ to 40 cents in the principal industries competing with Southern furniture manufacturers for labor.[28] Not only did employment for the industry as a whole increase the most in firms with the lowest average hourly earnings in 1937, where the statutory minima obviously had the greatest direct and immediate effect; but employment in the Southern plants increased 26 per cent, whereas it decreased slightly in competing Northern firms during the period (October, 1937 to February, 1941); and, within the South, employment expanded more than twice as fast in the lower-wage firms[29] whose wages were increased 10 per cent as it did in the higher-wage firms where the increase in wages was less than 2 per cent.[30]

Various factors were, of course, responsible for employment results so contrary to the presuppositions of conventional marginalism in such industries as men's cotton clothing and wood furniture. For the purposes of this paper there is no need to analyze individual cases where the results are so opposite to the expectations of marginal analysis and to assess the responsibility of each factor for those

practically eliminated, but in the work clothing and cotton pants branch, employment increased more than twice as fast in the South as in the North despite a reduction of more than 50 per cent in the North-South wage differential. See "Earnings in the Men's Cotton-Garment Industries, 1939 and 1941," *Mo. Lab. Rev.*, Vol. LV (August, 1942), p. 349.

[28] Seamless and full-fashioned hosiery, men's cotton clothing, and cotton textiles.

[29] Averaging under 35 cents an hour in 1937.

[30] The actual changes in hourly earnings and employment in 72 wood furniture plants from October, 1937 to February, 1941, were as follows:

Plants with average hourly earnings in 1937	Percentage increase in average hourly earnings, 1937 to 1941		Percentage increase in employment, 1937 to 1941	
	U. S.	South	U. S.	South
Under 32.5 cents	11.2%	10.2%	26.3%	29.1%
32.5 and under 35.0 cents	7.6	9.9	38.1	38.1
35.0 and under 37.5 cents	8.3	1.7	30.7	18.5
37.5 cents and over	2.4	1.7	0.4	16.8

Sources of data: *Earnings and Hours in the Furniture Industry, February 1941*, U. S. Bur. of Lab. Stat., Serial No. R. 1330, 1941, Table 3, p. 11, and *Minimum Wages in the Wood Furniture Manufacturing Industry*, Wage and Hour Division of U. S. Dept. of Labor, June, 1941, pp. 24–28. The employment increase for the South of 16.8 per cent was calculated from data in the latter publication on p. 28.

results.[31] Such data have been mentioned here merely to indicate that the replies of the Southern business executives discussed in this section do have some basis in fact and experience. Furthermore, furniture and men's cotton clothing concerns constitute half of the 43 Southern firms that gave full answers to a group of questions concerning the adjustments they would make to a sharp narrowing of the North-South wage differential in their industry.[32] The basic question was as follows:

Suppose that during the first 3 years after the defeat of Japan the average North-South wage differential in your industry should be cut in half, causing Southern wage rates in your line to rise relative to those of your competitors in the North. Assuming no other change in your costs and no decline in the nation's demand for the type of products you manufacture, how would your firm be likely to adjust to such a permanent 50-per-cent reduction in the North-South wage differential?

The executives were requested to rate each factor in terms of the relative importance or share in the total adjustment for which it would be responsible, the rating being in percentage terms on the basis of a composite of 100 per cent. The following list of factors was provided:

a. Install additional labor-saving machinery.
b. Improve efficiency through better production methods, organization, supervision, incentives, workloads, etc.
c. Change the price, quality, or kind of products manufactured.
d. Increase sales efforts so as to expand sales and production.
e. Reduce production by deliberately curtailing output.
f. Other adjustments (please specify).

The replying firms estimated their wage rates to be from 5 to 40 per cent under the average for comparable jobs in the North. The average for all replying was 18.2 per cent, so that the question involves,

[31] The notion that variations in geographic wage differentials and changes therein fairly accurately reflect geographic differences in labor effectiveness so that "efficiency-wages" are approximately the same for all regions or areas seems to be disproved by a North-South comparison that the author made between wages and labor efficiency in 41 firms with plants in both regions. See a forthcoming article, "Effectiveness of Factory Labor, South-North Comparisons," in the *Journal of Political Economy*.

[32] Ten firms declined to answer this set of questions on the ground that there was at present no differential, or only a negligible one, between their wage rate and average rates for comparable jobs in the North. Four of the 10 were in men's cotton clothing, in which previous figures have shown the North-South differential was rapidly reduced between 1939 and 1941.

on the average, an increase of 11 per cent in the wage scale of replying firms in the South, assuming no change in the wage level of their Northern competitors.

As the replying firms are mostly in industries that experienced some narrowing of the North-South wage differential under the National Recovery act and Fair Labor Standards act, their answers are founded on recent experience. Indeed, the replies are extremely helpful in interpreting that experience. They are summarized and classified by industry and labor-cost ratios in Table III. Also, Table III contains a summary for the 11 firms that estimate their wage rates to be from 25 to 40 per cent under the average rates of their Northern competitors for comparable jobs, and it is significant that the averages for those 11 firms (for which the question posits a selected wage increase of 17 to 33 per cent) are very similar to the averages for all 43 firms.[33]

The adjustment most frequently mentioned by the 43 firms was factor *b*, improvements in efficiency through better management, incentives, etc. Introduction of labor-saving machinery is the second most significant adjustment according to the results in Table III, and increased sales efforts ranks third. Price-product changes are considered the most important adjustment by some furniture concerns (3 of them placing sole stress on that factor),[34] but for the other firms such changes are considered of minor significance.[35]

It is especially noteworthy that deliberate curtailment of output, an adjustment stressed by conventional marginal theory, is mentioned by only 4 of the 43 firms.[36] Two of them, rating it at 10 per cent,

[33] The principal exception is that the factor of curtailing output has an average of 10 per cent for the 11 firms compared with an average of 4.1 per cent for all 43 firms. Responsibility for that result rests on one metal-working firm with a North-South wage differential estimated at 25 per cent, which rated this factor 100 per cent. Elimination of that firm would reduce the average for the factor of curtailing output to one per cent for the remaining 10 firms with large North-South wage differentials. The firm, subsequently discussed, failed to reports its ratio of labor costs to total costs so it is not included in the last group of figures in Table III.

[34] One furniture executive said he would enter a new field of manufacture of advanced products in furniture and veneers. However, another furniture manufacturer reported: "Such a change would affect us but very little as 90% of our market is in the South."

[35] "Other" adjustments were: "Use only higher skilled employees," "Replace inefficient labor with efficient labor," and "Several."

[36] Yet, reasoning on the basis of conventional theory, D. K. McKamy and John V. Van Sickle argue that elimination of the North-South wage differential

TABLE III — ADJUSTMENTS OF 43 SOUTHERN FIRMS TO SHARP NARROW-
ING OF NORTH-SOUTH WAGE DIFFERENTIALS, FACTORS
WEIGHTED ACCORDING TO PERCENTAGE OF IMPORTANCE

Classification of firms	a (labor-saving machinery)	b (improved methods and efficiency)	c (price-product changes)	d (increased sales efforts)	e (curtail output)	f (other)
Number of firms giving factor weight	35	36	19	31	4	4
Average weight per stressing firm	33%	36%	41%	29%	43%	20%
43-firm average of weights	26.1%	29.6%	17.5%	20.7%	4.1%	20%
Average for 14 furniture firms	19.6	23.2	34.3	17.9	.7	4.3
Average for 7 men's cotton clothing firms	24.3	40.0	17.1	18.6	—	—
Average for 10 metal-working firms	35.0	28.5	5.5	20.0	11.0	—
Average for 12 other firms	27.5	32.4	8.8	24.3	5.0	2.0
Average for 11 firms with North-South wage differential of 25 to 40%	25.0	30.5	10.9	20.0	10.0	3.6
Average for firms with labor-to-total cost ratios from						
40 to 60% (8 firms)	41.9	23.1	19.4	13.1	1.2	1.3
30 to 39% (8 firms)	33.1	28.7	14.4	15.0	6.3	2.5
21 to 29% (10 firms)	17.8	32.8	31.1	18.3	—	—
12 to 20% (9 firms)	22.8	36.2	7.8	26.7	1.0	5.5

had reported decreasing unit variable costs up to 100 per cent of plant
capacity; however, their percentage decreases in moving from 70 to
100 per cent of plant capacity totaled only 8 per cent in each instance.
The third firm, rating this factor 50 per cent, is the chemical concern

by government action would result in "an enormous and legislated growth of
unemployment," because "those enterprises in the areas of labor surplus which
are unable to earn enough money to pay the imposed wage would have to go
out of business or reduce employment to the point where the last workers
employed were worth as much as the imposed minimum." See *Statement of
D. K. McKamy and John V. Van Sickle with Regard to the Demand of the
Union for Elimination of Geographical Wage Differentials,* Company's Exhibit
No. 28, In the Matter of Carnegie-Illinois Steel Corporation, et al., and United
Steelworkers of America, Before the Steel Panel of the National War Labor
Board, Case No. 111-6230-D (14-1, et al.), June 7, 1944, p. 51.

in Table II that reported sharply increasing unit variable costs between 95 and 100 per cent of capacity and maximum profits in peacetime at 75 per cent of capacity. The fourth firm, a fabricator of steel structures and tanks with 125 employees, although reporting maximum profits at 100 per cent of capacity and decreasing unit variable costs between 70 and 100 per cent of capacity, places sole stress on this factor, making the following statement: "Volume of production would be reduced to small sales for a local market. The only reason we can now compete with the large Northern firms is due to the difference in wage scale. They have enormous advantages in freight rates and more skilled type of workman."

That business concerns stress item *b*, improved management and efficiency, may seem surprising to economists, who have generally reasoned as one replying executive, who stated: "Doing all these things is a continuous process with us. I don't see what the wage level has to do with it." Nevertheless, experience under the N.R.A. and the Fair Labor Standards act indicates that the spur of increased wages does lead to improved plant organization. An executive of one of the largest cotton-textile concerns in the South has testified that, under the N.R.A. requirement that the same wages be paid for 40 hours of work as formerly were paid for 55 hours, the firm's actual increase in labor costs was less than one-third of the expected or calculated increase, the difference being explained by "the utilization of improved machinery, better arrangement of processes and application of skilled labor, and the more adequate scheduling of the flow of production and better selection of raw materials."[37]

Greatest stress on factor *b*, better management and work procedures, is understandable in men's cotton clothing, where the possibilities of making savings through labor-reducing equipment are generally less than in metal-working plants, which gave the factor of additional labor-saving machinery the primary weight.[38] Also, as

[37] *Textile Industry, Findings and Opinion of the Administrator*, Wage and Hour Division, U. S. Dept. of Labor, September 29, 1939, p. 35.

[38] The possibilities of better management practices have frequently been emphasized in discussions of minimum-wage experience. See, for example, John F. Moloney, "Some Effects of the Federal Fair Labor Standards Act upon Southern Industry," *Southern Econ. Jour.*, Vol. IX (July, 1942), p. 22, and H. M. Douty, "Minimum Wage Regulation in the Seamless Hosiery Industry," *Southern Econ. Jour.*, Vol. VIII (October, 1941), p. 186.

In the seamless hosiery industry, with the introduction of 25-cent and 32½-cent minima in 1938 and 1940, respectively, employment declined more in the firms with average hourly earnings in the lowest wage classifications, largely due to increased use of labor-saving equipment in those firms (see Douty,

might be expected the firms with the highest rates of labor to total cost are the ones that place the most emphasis on new labor-saving machinery. Indeed, there is a notable inverse correlation between stress on that factor and the relative importance of labor in total costs. Exactly the reverse is true of the factor of increased sales efforts. The less stress is placed on sales efforts the larger is the percentage of labor in total costs. The implication is that large non-labor costs and increasing returns up to full capacity production bring to the fore the importance of keeping sales up when profits begin to be squeezed.

Economists brought up on the conventional theory may discount the stress placed by the business executives on increased sales efforts, considering it to be an irrational and uneconomic reaction to a wage increase. Previous data on the relationship between rates of output and unit variable costs indicate, however, that such stress on increased sales efforts may have some rationality. It may help to raise and retain output near capacity operations. Data at the beginning of this section indicate that expanding sales, output, and employment may, at times, be one of the results in firms most affected by wage increases. Business men are acutely aware of the fact that unit costs vary with output, that wage rates which seem extremely burdensome at half-capacity operations may not seem unduly high as full-capacity production is approached. Unlike economists, business executives tend to think of costs and profits as dependent upon the rate of output, rather than the reverse (the rate of output as dependent upon the level of cost).

V

This paper raises grave doubts as to the validity of conventional marginal theory and the assumptions on which its rests. Admittedly the data used are imperfect and are based, for the most part, on opinions of business executives. Many of the replying executives are, however, heads of "small" businesses in highly competitive industries, so that they are good test cases for the theory. There may, of course, be questions concerning the representativeness of the samples, the completeness of the data, the content and character of the questions, etc. It may be argued, if somewhat unconvincingly, that business executives as a group do not learn from past experience and do not know their own businesses. Nevertheless, the answers of the replying

Southern Econ. Jour., Vol. VIII, pp. 183–89). However, there is no evidence that total output or sales of those low-wage firms, most affected by the wage minima, experienced any decline relative to the average for the industry.

executives are sufficiently consistent, firm by firm, and so overwhelmingly support certain reasonable conclusions that there can be little doubt about the correctness of the general results.

While awaiting the fruits of further investigation and analysis, the following tentative conclusions can be drawn from the data contained in this paper:

1. Market demand is far more important than wage rates in determining a firm's volume of employment.[39] Indeed, for employment determination, market demand is considered by business executives to be almost five times as important as all other factors combined,[40] and the wage level or changes in wages are considered to be no more important in determining a firm's employment than the level of non-labor costs and changes in such non-labor costs.

2. Most manufacturing concerns apparently are considered by their executives to be operating at decreasing unit variable costs all along the scale between 70 and 100 per cent of plant capacity. Consequently, it is seldom practical for a firm to curtail output (and, therefore, employment) simply in response to an increase in wage rates.

3. In modern manufacturing, a firm's level of costs per unit of product is influenced considerably by its scale of output; the reverse, as assumed by conventional marginalism, is not generally true.

4. Interregional firms, except in rare cases, do not adjust their use of labor and capital equipment to compensate for sectional differences in wage rates. For many manufacturing concerns it is not feasible, or would prove too costly, to shift the proportion of productive factors in response to current changes in wages, in the manner suggested by marginal analysis.

5. The practical problems involved in applying marginal analysis to the multi-process operations of a modern plant seem insuperable, and business executives rightly consider marginalism impractical as an operating principle in such manufacturing establishments.

6. Of the three adjustments stressed by business executives to meet a rise in wages relative to those paid by competitors, two — better

[39] The 56 replying firms gave market demand an average rating of 87.5 compared with an average of 3.8 for the level of wages or changes therein, which, taken literally, would mean that market demand is more than 26 times as important as wage rates in determining the volume of employment of a firm.

[40] The relative importance of market demand was assessed by the executives of 56 firms at 82.5 compared with 17.5 for all other factors influencing a firm's employment. The ratio is 65 to 35 for the 28 firms rating two or more factors (see Table I).

management practices and increased sales efforts — are neglected by conventional marginalism; whereas the adjustment stressed by marginalism — curtailment of output — is considered so unimportant and exceptional as to be mentioned in only one out of every 11 replies. Indeed, experience seems to indicate that, on an individual-firm basis, the adjustments considered important by the business executives may, at times, even result in larger firm employment at a higher wage level.

These tentative conclusions indicate a new direction for investigations of employment relationships and equilibrating adjustments in individual firms.

FRITZ MACHLUP

Marginal Analysis and Empirical Research[*]

Machlup acknowledges that business leaders do not always act like the "economic man" of marginal analysis. He admits that they usually do not consciously think as marginalists, but nevertheless, if they seek to maximize profits, how well they succeed will be determined by how closely they act like marginalists.

Machlup questioned that the low rating Lester's respondents gave to wage rate levels and changes in determining the volume of employment substantiated the opinion that the firms neither thought nor acted according to marginal principles. He points out that product demand, reported as the most important factor, is just as important an element in marginal analysis as wage changes. An increase in demand or equivalent decline in wages, for example, would have equal influence in raising employment.

In addition, Machlup notes a seeming contradiction in Lester's questionnaire responses. In answer to the question regarding pro-

* Reprinted by permission of the author from the *American Economic Review*, XXXVI (September 1946), pp. 519–528, 533–538, 547–554.

duction techniques, almost all the firms having northern and southern plants stated that lower southern wages did not lead them to utilize production methods that would employ more labor relative to capital in their southern, compared with their northern, plants. This suggested an inflexibility in the substitutability of factors of production. However, in responding to how they would react to a relative rise in southern wages, these same firms gave the introduction of labor-saving machinery a very high rating as an adjustment to this situation. This latter response indicates a degree of flexibility in factor substitution, consistent with marginal theory, not suggested by the answer to the former question.

If this small sample of Machlup's points suggests to the student that his article is strongly critical of the antimarginalist position, it must be emphasized that Machlup is not merely defending an individual point of view, but one of the principal postulates of economic theory—the applicability of marginal analysis to economic behavior.

CERTAIN critics of "conventional" economic theory from time to time voice surprise at the general acceptance of marginalism and at "the confidence of the textbook writers in the validity of the marginal analysis."[1] They disapprove of allowing the principle of marginalism to play the rôle of a fundamental postulate in the teaching of economics.

Marginalism Implied in the Economic Principle

These critics would probably revolt against all those definitions of economics which contain marginalism as an implicit criterion. Marginalism, as the logical process of "finding a maximum," is clearly implied in the so-called *economic principle* — striving to achieve with given means a maximum of ends.

Economics in a narrow sense is confined to such aspects of conduct as can be explained with reference to the principles of maximizing satisfaction, income, or profit. Under definitions of this sort any deviations from the marginal principle would be extra-economic.

---

[1] Richard A. Lester, "Shortcomings of Marginal Analysis for Wage-Employment Problems," *Am. Econ. Rev.*, Vol. XXXVI, No. 1 (Mar., 1946), p. 63.

Yet, to refuse to deal with any type of business conduct that cannot qualify by the strict standards of marginalism may justly be regarded as a lazy man's excuse. If certain types of business conduct can be found in reality with regularity and consistency, it is undoubtedly desirable to analyze them regardless of their "economic rationale."[2] And if some of these allegedly "non-economic" aspects of conduct can be explained within the conceptual framework of economics, one may prefer definitions which admit behavior types not strictly subject to marginal analysis among the proper subject matter of economic theory.

Interpretation of Business Behavior

To recognize the study of certain types of merely "traditional" conduct as legitimately within the province of economic theory is one thing; it is another to accept as correct the interpretations of business behavior offered by the critics of marginal analysis. Unable to see how marginal analysis can be applied to their material, these critics have concluded that marginalism should be discarded. It can be shown, however, that the alleged "inapplicability" of marginal analysis is often due to a failure to understand it, to faulty research techniques, or to mistaken interpretations of "findings."

This is not to deny that a goodly portion of all business behavior may be non-rational, thoughtless, blindly repetitive, deliberately traditional, or motivated by extra-economic objectives. But the material thus far presented as the result of empirical research has not proved what the analysts intended to prove. In some instances their findings were the result of careful research, based on a thorough knowledge of economic theory, but their interpretations were still questionable. In other instances the whole approach of the research project was so faulty that the findings as well as the interpretations are all but worthless except as targets for critical discussion.

I. MARGINAL ANALYSIS OF THE SINGLE FIRM

Any attempt to "test" marginalist theory through empirical research presupposes full understanding of the theory. It is necessary to know precisely what the theory says, what it implies, and what it intends to do. Since it has been developed gradually over a period of more

---

[2] Cf. the admonition that "if an economist finds a procedure widely established in fact, he ought to regard it with more respect than he would be inclined to give in the light of his own analytic method." R. F. Harrod, "Price and Cost in Enterpreneurs' Policy," Oxford Economic Papers, No. 2 (1939), p. 7.

than a century,[3] it will not suffice to take any particular writer as
one's authority or any particular exposition as one's text. Earlier
versions lack the necessary refinements and methodological founda-
tions; later formulations often take for granted necessary assumptions
or qualifications made in previous expositions. To criticize the theory
because of the errors and omissions in any treatise, however representative, is unfair.

The following statement of essential elements in the marginalist
analysis of the single business firm attempts merely to give major
emphasis to points often overlooked or misunderstood.

The Determination of Output and Employment

The theory of the "equilibrium of the single firm" is not as ambitious
as is often believed. It does not attempt to give all the reasons why
a given firm makes the type or quality of product which it makes;
why it produces the output that it produces; why it employs the
workers that it employs; or why it charges the prices that it charges.
It is probably an understatement of the importance of the historical
situation when Hall and Hitch modestly remark: "There is usually
some element in the prices ruling at any time which can only be
explained in the light of the history of the industry."[4] The phrase
"usually some element" does not do justice to the part played by historical antecedents in the determination of product, output, employment, and prices. The rôle of the past in shaping the actual conditions under which the firm operates, in developing the routine of its
responses to changes in conditions, and in impressing it with experiences which have taught it to size up and anticipate these changes
as the basis for its decisions — this rôle is by no means denied by
marginal analysis. The rôle of the past in the process of adjusting
the present to the anticipated future is essential in all theory of human
conduct. It is implied in the very attempt of constructing a pattern
of behavior of the single firm.

Instead of giving a complete explanation of the "determination"
of output, prices, and employment by the firm, marginal analysis
really intends to explain the effects which certain *changes* in conditions may have upon the actions of the firm. What kind of changes
may cause the firm to raise prices? to increase output? to reduce

[3] Cournot was among the earlier expositors of marginal analysis of the single
firm.

[4] R. L. Hall and C. J. Hitch, "Price Theory and Business Behavior," *Oxford
Economic Papers*, No. 2 (1939), p. 33.

employment? What conditions may influence the firm to continue with the same prices, output, employment, in the face of actual or anticipated changes? Economic theory, static as well as dynamic, is essentially a theory of adjustment to change. The concept of equilibrium is a tool in this theory of change; the marginal calculus is its dominating principle.

A. Marginal Revenue and Cost of Output

Subjectivity of Cost and Revenue

The proposition that the firm will attempt to equate marginal cost and marginal revenue is logically implied in the assumption that the firm will attempt to maximize its profit (or minimize its losses). It should hardly be necessary to mention that all the relevant magnitudes involved — cost, revenue, profit — are subjective — that is, perceived or fancied by the men whose decisions or actions are to be explained (the business men) — rather than "objective" — that is, calculated by disinterested men who are observing these actions from the outside and are explaining them (statisticians and economists as theorists — not as consultants).

The marginal cost that guides the producer is the addition to his total cost which he expects would be caused by added production. An outside observer, if he had expert knowledge of the production techniques and full insight into the cost situation of the producing firm, might arrive at a different, "objective" figure of the firm's marginal cost; but what the observer thinks is not necessarily the same as what the producer thinks. The producer's actual decision is based on what he himself thinks; it is based on "subjective" cost expectations.

One may perhaps assume that the producer is intensely interested in knowing his cost and that, in general, he has the experience which enables him to know it. Yet one must not assume that all producers "really" know their cost in the sense in which an efficiency expert would determine it; several of them may lack the interest or experience; they may not find it worth their while to dig too deeply into the mysteries of their business. (After all, we know that there are good business men and bad, and that the majority is somewhere between good and bad.) But this does not invalidate the proposition that the producer is guided by marginal cost.[5]

The same thing is true with regard to price expectations and sales expectations. It is the "demand as seen by the seller" from

[5] One may wish, of course, to qualify any social implications of the proposition once the subjective character of the relevant cost data is recognized.

which his revenue expectations stem. The increase in demand which is relevant in the analysis of the firm need not be "the real thing"; it may precede an "actual" increase in demand, lag behind it, or be entirely imaginary. The business man does what he does on the basis of what *he* thinks, regardless of whether you agree with him or not.

Marginal analysis of the firm should not be understood to imply anything but subjective estimates, guesses and hunches.

The Range of Price and Output Variations

Beginning students of economics who watch their instructor draw demand and cost curves covering half the blackboard may be misled into believing that the business man is supposed to visualize the possibilities of producing and selling amounts of output ranging from almost zero up to two or three times the amounts that he is currently producing and selling; that the business man is supposed to figure out how much he might be able to sell at prices several times as high as the current price, and how much at prices only one-half or one-third as high. The curve draftsman, indeed, seems to ascribe extraordinary powers of imagination to the business wizards.

Misunderstandings of this sort, and erroneous criticisms of marginal analysis, could be avoided if it were made clear to the students that the length of the curves, *i.e.*, the wide range they cover, was chiefly designed to enable those in the back rows of the class room to make out what goes on on the blackboard; and to permit them to practice curve analysis without using magnifying glasses. The range of possibilities — prices, sales, outputs — which a business man may have in mind is probably quite narrow. Rarely will a business man bother pondering the probable effects of a price increase or cut by 50 per cent; but he may easily think about what a 10 or 15 per cent price change might do to his sales; or what discount it might take to land some additional orders.

The principles of analysis are not altered by the realization that the alternatives which business men weigh concerning prices or production volumes cover a much more moderate range than the curves which teachers of economics draw to depict the pattern of marginal calculus.

The Time-Range of Anticipations

In view of the known attempts to derive statistical cost curves from accounting data — which of necessity refer to conditions of the past — it is important to mention that the marginal cost and marginal revenue concepts in the analysis of the equilibrium of the firm refer to expectations of future conditions. To be sure, past experience is always in the background of anticipations of the future, and past accounting records may form a firm point of departure for evaluating prospective and hypothetical cost and revenue figures. But anticipations alone are the relevant variables in the marginal calculus of the firm.

What is the time-range of the significant anticipations? How far into the future do they reach, and what period, if any, is given special emphasis? Is tomorrow more important than next year or several years hence? Is it the "short run" or the "long run" which controls current action?

When a firm wishes to increase production, it usually has a choice of expanding the equipment and productive capacity of its plant or of stepping up the output of the existing plant with unchanged equipment. If productive capacity is already well utilized, the marginal cost of producing larger outputs will be higher in the existing establishment with unchanged equipment than in an establishment with adjusted, increased equipment. If several degrees of adjustment in the productive equipment are possible, several marginal cost functions will be "given" and several different outputs will be "the equilibrium output" under given sales expectations.

To cope with these problems economists have made the distinction between the "short period," assuming no adaptation of equipment, and the "long period," assuming complete adaptation of equipment. Students often believe that the latter period is called "long" because it takes a long time to expand the plant. This need not be the case. A better understanding of the concepts might be achieved by associating the degree of planned plant adjustment with the length of time for which the changed production volume is expected to be maintained. If an increased demand is expected to prevail for a short period only, it will not pay to invest in plant expansion, and "short-run cost" will determine output. On the other hand, if demand is expected to continue at the higher level for a sufficiently long period, an expansion of the establishment will be considered a profitable investment, and "long-run cost" will determine output. Needless to say, many intermediate periods, that is, several degrees of plant adjustment with different marginal cost conditions, may exist.

On the basis of this reasoning one will recognize it as a misunderstanding to argue that short-run cost is of controlling influence on the ground that we always live and work in the short period. The duration for which demand conditions are expected to prevail will determine the relevant "period" of cost anticipations. Of course, this relevance is again subjectively determined, not by the "objective" judgment of the economist.

The time-range of the anticipations with regard to the demand and selling outlook is subject to similar considerations. It is a mistake to think that the relevant "period" for demand and marginal revenue expectations is determined by the length of time it takes for today's production to reach the market. If a price reduction is apt to spoil the market for a long time to come, or a price increase to harm customer loyalty, the effects on future profits will hardly be neglected in considering current actions. If a firm were to regard a certain price change as a desirable step for the time being, but feared that a later reversal might be difficult or costly, it would weigh this anticipated future cost or loss against the short-run benefit.

Anticipations of this sort, complementary or competing with one another, are not exceptions to marginal analysis but are part and parcel of it. To be sure, when an instructor teaches graphical analysis, he will do well to abstract from complicated cost and revenue anticipations and to concentrate on those that can be neatly packed away in geometric curves.

The Numerical Definiteness of the Estimates

The geometric curves and arithmetic schedules by which the instructor presents marginal cost and marginal revenue of the firm seem to leave no room for doubt that these anticipations take the form of estimates of definite numerical values. While this may be necessary for teaching purposes, it should not mislead the student into believing that every action of the business man is in fact the result of a conscious decision, made after careful calculations of differential revenue and cost.

Business men do not always "calculate" before they make decisions, and they do not always "decide" before they act. For they think that they know their business well enough without having to make repeated calculations; and their actions are frequently routine. But routine is based on principles which were once considered and decided upon and have then been frequently applied with decreasing need for conscious choices.[6] The feeling that calculations are not

[6] Discussing the difference between "routine behavior" and "genuine decisions," Dr. Katona explains with regard to routine actions that "principles, well understood in their original context, tend to be carried over from one situation to another," George Katona "Psychological Analysis of Business Decisions and Expectations," *American Economic Review,* Vol. XXXVI, No. 1 (March, 1946), p. 49. Genuine decisions are made when expectations "change radically." *Ibid.,* p. 53.

always necessary is usually based upon an ability to size up a situation without reducing its dimensions to definite numerical values.[7]

The business man who is persuaded to accept a large order with a price discount or some other concession usually weighs the probability that he will have to make the same concession to his other customers. This is one of the business man's considerations included in the "calculation" of marginal revenue. In order to explain this to the student, or to reduce it to curves and schedules, the economics teacher makes "exact" calculations; in order to make up his mind whether to take or reject the order, the business man ordinarily needs no arithmetic, mental or written, and indeed needs no concrete figures. Yet his reasoning or his routine behavior is most conveniently analyzed in terms of marginal revenue.

Where the marginal revenue is negative, that is to say, where gross receipts after accepting the additional order (with the price concession) would be smaller than without it, no further consideration is necessary. But if the dollar volume of sales can be increased by accepting the order (taking full account of all repercussions on future marketing possibilities), the business man must take another step in his reasoning: will it pay to make more sales in view of the additional cost of producing the larger output? If conditions have not changed, he will not have to make new calculations; if changes have occurred or are expected, some figuring may be required. But it is a type of figuring for which usually no accounting records are consulted, no memoranda prepared and of which no records are made. Often the business man can do this "figuring" in his head; if not, he may take a piece of scrap paper, jot down a few round numbers, reach his conclusion, and throw the paper in the waste basket.

The theorist's contention that such reasoning is typically based either on additional cost or on total cost — and hence most conveniently described in terms of marginal cost — is contradicted by certain empirical researchers who claim that most business men calculate on the basis of average cost even if they lose money by doing so. With this contradiction we shall deal later.

Non-Pecuniary Considerations

Marginal analysis of the equilibrium of the single firm rests on the assumption that the business firm attempts to maximize its profits.

---

[7] Although I do not know either the width or length of my automobile, I am quite capable of making adequate comparisons between these magnitudes and the space between two parked cars, which I estimate again without thinking of feet, inches, or any numbers.

To make this assumption is not to deny that the men who run a business may be motivated also by other considerations.

That a business man is motivated by considerations other than the maximization of money profits does not necessarily make his conduct "uneconomic." The economic theorist finds no difficulty in fitting into the pattern of "economic" conduct (that is, into the conceptual scheme of consistent maximization of satisfaction within a given preference system) the householder and consumer who makes donations to friends or the church; or the seller of labor services who chooses a badly-paying but less strenuous job in preference to one that pays more but calls for more exertion. Likewise, there is nothing essentially "uneconomic" in the conduct of a business man who chooses to pay higher prices for raw material purchased from a fraternity brother, or to sell at a special discount to members of his church, or who refrains from embarking on a promising expansion of his business because he prefers an easier life.

There are economic theorists who would include considerations of this sort among the data for the marginal calculus of the firm. The satisfaction from favoring his friends through higher purchase prices or lower selling prices is a special reward or "revenue" to the business man; he may ask himself how much it is worth to him, and we may conceivably add it to his revenue curve. To give up an easier life, expend greater efforts and increase his worries are among the business man's "costs" when he considers an expansion of his business; we may conceivably add it to his "cost" curve. Any number and type of non-pecuniary sacrifices and rewards could thus be included, at some sort of "money equivalent," among the costs and revenues that make up the profits of the firm: the marginal calculus of the firm would become all-inclusive.

It seems to be methodologically sounder if we do not reduce the non-pecuniary satisfactions and dissatisfactions (utilities and disutilities) of the business man to money terms and do not try to make them part of the profit maximization scheme of the firm. If *whatever* a business man does is explained by the principle of profit maximization — because he does what he likes to do, and he likes to do what maximizes the sum of his pecuniary and non-pecuniary profits — the analysis acquires the character of a system of definitions and tautologies, and loses much of its value as an explanation of reality. It is preferable to separate the non-pecuniary factors of business conduct from those which are regular items in the formation of money profits.

This methodological controversy is not too important. Not much depends on whether non-pecuniary considerations of the business man are translated into money terms or, instead, treated as exceptions and qualifications in the explanation of typical business conduct. The purpose of the analysis of the firm is not to explain all actions of each and every firm in existence; we are satisfied if we can explain certain strong tendencies in a representative sector of business. The chief aim of the analysis, moreover, is to show the probable effects of certain changes; if the direction in which output or price is likely to move as a result of a certain change in "data" is not affected by the existence and strength of non-pecuniary factors in business conduct, their inclusion in or exclusion from the marginal analysis of the firm is not a crucial matter.

As a matter of fact, the nature, strength and effects of non-pecuniary considerations in business behavior are problems that need to be investigated. One may presume that producing larger production volumes, paying higher wage rates, or charging lower product prices than would be compatible with a maximum of money profits may involve for the business man a gain in social prestige or a certain measure of inner satisfaction.[8] It is not impossible that considerations of this sort substantially weaken the forces believed to be at work on the basis of a strictly pecuniary marginal calculus.

During the war we were able to observe that patriotism was a strong force in the production policy of American business. There can be no doubt that many firms produced far beyond the point of highest money profits. To be sure, they made large profits, but in many instances they could have made still more money without the last, particularly expensive, portions of output. Their conduct was not defined by the principles of maximization of money profits.[9]

Another of the possibly important qualifications in the analysis of the firm refers to the conflict of interests between the hired managers and the owners of the business. The interest of the former in

---

[8] A gain in social prestige may sometimes increase the good will of a firm on which it expects to cash in later. If such a gain is an aim of the firm's policy, it should be treated as a part of its pecuniary considerations. For example, a firm may grant extraordinarily high wage rates as a part of its selling and advertising expense; that is to say, it may hope that its "generous labor policy" will make its products more popular. A portion of current labor cost of the firm would then properly be allocated to future rather than current output.

[9] Observance of laws and regulations presents a special problem for the analysis of business conduct. It will depend on business morals whether prohibited, unlawful alternatives may be regarded as definitely excluded and therefore non-existent; or whether they may be considered as possibilities subject only to certain peculiar risks. Assume, for example, that a price ceiling is fixed for the sale of a product, and fines are provided for violations. To the business

inordinately large outlays or investments may be capable of description in terms of a pecuniary calculus, but it is not maximization of the firm's profits which serves here as the standard of conduct. Maximization of salaries and bonuses of professional managers may constitute a standard of business conduct different from that implied in the customary marginal analysis of the firm. The extent to which the two standards would result in sharply different action under otherwise similar conditions is another open question in need of investigation. At this juncture we know only that a qualification must be made. How much it may modify the results of marginal analysis of the single firm we do not know.

*   *   *

Subjectivity, Range, Concreteness

Almost everything that has been said in earlier sections concerning the meaning of marginal revenue and marginal cost of output holds true, *mutatis mutandis*, in regard to the meaning of marginal productivity and marginal cost of input. More specifically, we should emphasize that

(1) the concepts are to be understood as referring to subjective estimates and conjectures;

(2) the range of imagined variations of the magnitudes in question may be rather narrow;

(3) the time-range of the relevant anticipations will depend on the circumstances of each case and will rarely be confined to the short run;

(4) the estimates need not be reduced to definite numerical values;

(5) non-pecuniary considerations may effectively compete with those pertaining to the maximization of money profits.

It is probably unnecessary to expatiate again on these points in connection with marginal productivity analysis. Only on the subject of numerical definiteness does further discussion seem advisable, especially in view of what was said above about the concept of mar-

man who is unconditionally law-abiding the ceiling price is the only possible price, regardless of how insistently some of his customers may tempt him with higher bids. To the business man, however, who abides by the law only because of the risk of being found out and fined, "demand prices" above the ceiling are real possibilities and the risks of penalties are additions to cost or deductions from revenue. If the sanctions for violations include jail sentences, the risk becomes largely non-pecuniary and it is up to the potential violator, or to the theorizing economist, whether or not that risk will be "converted" into money terms. Black-market prices are in part the result of such risk conversions.

ginal net revenue productivity. The process by which this magnitude may be derived, involving seven separate "steps" and at least as many variables, is rather formidable. If this analytical pattern were taken as a realistic description in photographic likeness of the actual reasoning of the typical employer, the employer would have to be endowed with talents which only few possess in reality.

An analogy may explain the apparent contradiction.

The "Extreme Difficulty of Calculating"

What sort of considerations are behind the routine decision of the driver of an automobile to overtake a truck proceeding ahead of him at slower speed? What factors influence his decision? Assume that he is faced with the alternative of either slowing down and staying behind the truck or of passing it before a car which is approaching from the opposite direction will have reached the spot. As an experienced driver he somehow takes into account (a) the speed at which the truck is going, (b) the remaining distance between himself and the truck, (c) the speed at which he is proceeding, (d) the possible acceleration of his speed, (e) the distance between him and the car approaching from the opposite direction, (f) the speed at which that car is approaching; and probably also the condition of the road (concrete or dirt, wet or dry, straight or winding, level or uphill), the degree of visibility (light or dark, clear or foggy), the condition of the tires and brakes of his car, and — let us hope — his own condition (fresh or tired, sober or alcoholized) permitting him to judge the enumerated factors.

Clearly, the driver of the automobile will not "measure" the variables; he will not "calculate" the time needed for the vehicles to cover the estimated distances at the estimated rates of speed; and, of course, none of the "estimates" will be expressed in numerical values. Even so, without measurements, numerical estimates or calculations, he will in a routine way do the indicated "sizing-up" of the total situation. He will not break it down into its elements. Yet a "theory of overtaking" would have to include all these elements (and perhaps others besides) and would have to state how changes in any of the factors were likely to affect the decisions or actions of the driver.[10] The "extreme difficulty of calculating,"[11] the fact that "it

[10] Very cautious drivers are apt to work with so wide safety margins that small changes in the "variables" may not affect the actions. Timid souls may refuse to pass at all when another car is in sight.

[11] Lester, *Am. Econ. Rev.*, Vol. XXXVI, No. 1, p. 72.

would be utterly impractical"[12] to attempt to work out and ascertain the exact magnitudes of the variables which the theorist alleges to be significant, show merely that the *explanation* of an action must often include steps of reasoning which the acting individual himself does not *consciously* perform (because the action has become routine) and which perhaps he would never be *able* to perform in scientific exactness (because such exactness is not necessary in everyday life). To call, on these grounds, the theory "invalid," "unrealistic" or "inapplicable" is to reveal failure to understand the basic methodological constitution of most social sciences.

Imagine an empirical researcher attempting to test by a naïve questionnaire method the "theory of overtaking," questioning hundreds of drivers about their ability to estimate distances and speed, and to calculate the relevant time intervals and the degrees in which a small change in any one of the variables affected the result. Would he not obtain the most hopeless assortment of answers? Would not these answers support the conclusion that the assumptions of the theorists had been wrong and that one must look for other explanations? Yet I can hardly believe that any sensible person would deny the relevance of the enumerated variables and would contend, for example, that speed and distance of the approaching automobile could not have been taken into account by the driver passing the truck, because he was not good in mathematics.[13]

The Analysis of Change Needs No Exactness

The business man who equates marginal net revenue productivity and marginal factor cost when he decides how many to employ need not engage in higher mathematics, geometry, or clairvoyance. Ordinarily he would not even consult with his accountant or efficiency expert in order to arrive at his decision; he would not make any tests or formal calculations; he would simply rely on his sense or his "feel" of the situation. There is nothing very exact about this sort of estimate. On the basis of hundreds of previous experiences of a similar nature the business man would "just know," in a vague and rough way, whether or not it would pay him to hire more men.

---

[12] Lester, *ibid.,* p. 75.

[13] Driving at night, when he has nothing to go by except the size and brilliance of the headlights of the approaching cars, the experienced driver becomes conscious of the fact that in daytime he has better ways of sizing up their speed and distance. With reduced visibility he will "calculate" with greater safety margins.

The subjectivity of his judgments is obvious. Just as different drivers may reach different conclusions about the advisability of passing another car under given "objective" conditions, different business men will have different "hunches" in a given situation. The subordinates or partners of the man who makes a decision may sharply disagree with him; they may see the situation quite differently. They may be more optimistic about the possibilities of obtaining more orders with only slight price concessions or through increased sales efforts (which would raise both the marginal revenue and marginal productivity curves drawn by the theorist to characterize their considerations). Or they may be more certain about the technical possibility of achieving a larger output by certain production methods (which would lower the marginal cost curve, and could raise or lower the marginal productivity curves). Some decision, usually a routine decision without debate, is made, or at least some action is taken; and the decision or action is necessarily affected by the business man's conjectures concerning sales possibilities and production possibilities.

The way in which changes in the essential variables will affect the probable decisions and actions of the business man is not much different if the curves which the theorist draws to depict their conjectures are a little higher or lower, steeper or flatter. These curves are helpful to the student of economics in figuring out the probable effects of change — in learning in what direction output, prices and employment are likely to be altered, and under what circumstances increases or decreases are likely to be drastic or negligible. Better markets or higher costs are likely to affect business men of different vision or daring in rather similar ways; and any differences can be conveniently "typed" in terms of shapes, positions and shifts of the curves into which the theorist condenses the business men's conjectures.

Equipped with this understanding of the meaning and purposes of marginal analysis, we may proceed to a discussion of the findings of empirical research which purportedly failed to verify it — or by which it was deemed to be contradicted and disproved.

II. EMPIRICAL RESEARCH ON THE SINGLE FIRM

There is not as yet available any large amount of material derived from systematic empirical research on the business conduct of the single firm. But almost everybody interested in these questions has had occasional conversations with business men, and the impressions gained from such inquiries into the business men's experiences often form an empirical basis for the doubt which so-called "realistic" critics entertain of "theoretical" analysis.

I submit that the few systematic and the many casual researchers have often been misled by pitfalls of semantics and terminology and by a naïve acceptance of rationalizations in lieu of genuine explanations of actions.

Economists' Vocabulary and Business Language

The vast majority of business men have never heard of expressions such as elasticity of demand or supply, sloping demand curves, marginal revenue, marginal cost. If they do not know the words or the concepts, how can they be supposed to think in these terms? A scattered few of the men may have been exposed to such words and ideas in half-forgotten college courses, but they have found in practice they had no use for a vocabulary unknown to their associates, superiors, subordinates, and fellow business men. Thus the most essential terms in which economists explain business conduct do not exist in the business man's vocabulary. Does this not prove that the explanations are unrealistic or definitely false?

Only an inexperienced researcher could draw such a conclusion. The technical terms used in the explanation of an action need not have any part in the thinking of the acting individual. A mental process in everyday life may often be most conveniently described for scientific purposes in a language which is quite foreign to the process itself.

To ask a business man about the "elasticity of demand" for his product is just as helpful as inquiring into the customs of an indigenous Fiji Islander by interviewing him in the King's English. But with a little ingenuity it is possible to translate ideas from the business man's language into that of the economist, and *vice versa*. Questions such as "Do you think you might sell more of this product if you cut the price by 10 per cent?" or "How much business do you think you would lose if you raised your price by 10 per cent?" will evoke intelligent answers in most cases provided the questions are readily reformulated and adapted to the peculiarities of the particular man and his business. Often it will be necessary to know a good deal of the technology, customs and jargon of the trade, and even of the personal idiosyncrasies of the men, before one can ask the right questions. A set formulation of questions will hardly fit any large number of business men in different fields and, hence, questionnaires to be filled out by them will rarely yield useful results.

Rationalizations of Decisions or Actions

Psychologists will readily confirm that statements by interviewed individuals about the motives and reasons for their actions are unreliable or at least incomplete. Even if a person tries to reconstruct for himself in his memory the motives and reasons for one of his past actions, he will usually end up with a rationalization full of afterthoughts that may make his actions appear more plausible to himself. Explanations given to an interviewer or investigator are still more likely to be rationalizations in terms that may make the particular actions appear plausible and justified to the inquirer. In order to be understood (and respected) the interviewed person will often choose for his "explanations" patterns of reasoning which he believes to be recognized as "sound" and "fair" by others. Most of these rationalizations may be subjectively honest and truthful. It takes an experienced analyst to disentangle actual from imaginary reasons, and to separate relevant from irrelevant data, and essential from decorative bits of the information furnished. Written replies to questionnaires are hopelessly inadequate for such purposes.

Questions of business policy are particularly difficult objects of inquiry because the business man usually is anxious to show by his answers that he is intelligent, well informed, and fair. The standards of fairness and business ethics to which he wishes to conform are often those which he believes are accepted by his lawyers, accountants, customers, competitors, fellow citizens, economists and whatnot. Only through detailed discussions of different situations and decisions, actual as well as hypothetical, will an investigator succeed in bringing out true patterns of conduct of the individual business man.

*   *   *

B. Marginal Productivity and Wage

Empirical research designed to verify or disprove marginal productivity theory in the analysis of input of the individual firm is beset with difficulties. Few systematic endeavors have been made and none has led to any suggestion, however vague or tentative, of an alternative theory. Whereas in certain price research projects those who felt compelled to reject the marginal theory have advanced the average-cost theory of pricing as a substitute, no substitute theory has been forthcoming from those who decried marginal productivity theory.

Statistical Research

Empirical research on cost, price and output of the individual firm has resulted in several interesting attempts to derive marginal cost functions from statistical data; and also in one or two attempts to derive price elasticities of demand for a firm's products. But nobody, to my knowledge, has ever undertaken to construct from actual data a marginal net revenue productivity curve for a given type of labor employed by a firm. The difficulties are formidable and, since the raw material for the calculations could not come from any records or documents but merely from respondent's guesses of a purely hypothetical nature, the results might not be much more "authentic" than the schedules made up by textbook writers for arithmetical illustrations.

Statistical studies of the relationship between wage rates and employment in large samples of individual firms or industries would be nearly useless because we have no way of eliminating the simultaneous effects of several other significant variables, especially those of a psychological nature. An increase in wage rates may have very different effects depending on whether the employer (1) (a) has foreseen it, (b) is surprised by it; (2) (a) reacts quickly to it, (b) reacts slowly to it; (3) (a) expects it to be reversed soon, (b) expects it to be maintained, (c) expects it to be followed by further increases; (4) (a) assumes it to be confined to his firm, (b) assumes it to affect also his competitors, (c) believes it to be part of a nation-wide trend; (5) connects it with an inflationary development; or is influenced by any other sort and number of anticipations. Most of these moods and anticipations can be translated by the economist into certain shapes or shifts of the marginal productivity functions of the firms; but since the researchers cannot ascertain or evaluate these conjectural "data" for the large number of firms contained in a representative sample, statistical investigations of the wage-employment relation of individual firms are not likely to yield useful results.

Questionnaire on Employment

It has been pointed out why the method of mailed questionnaires without supporting interviews is hopelessly inadequate for empirical studies of business conduct. Even the most intelligently devised set of questions would not assure reliable and significant answers. Questions designed to achieve the necessary separation of variables would be so complicated and call for so high a degree of "abstract thinking" on the part of the questioned business men that questionnaires of this sort would be too much of an imposition, and coöperation would be too small. Although the questions in Professor Lester's research project on employment did not even approach these standards, he received only 56 usable replies from 430 manufacturers whom he had asked to fill out his questionnaires.[14]

Professor Lester's questionnaires suffered not merely from the inherent weaknesses of the method but also from defects in formulation. These defects were so serious that even the most complete, reliable and intelligent answers could not have yielded significant findings. The business men were asked to rate the "importance" of several factors determining the volume of employment in their firms. No explanation was given whether this importance of a variable — that is, I presume, its responsibility for changes in the employment volume — should refer to (a) the frequency of its variations, (b) the extent of its variations, or (c) the effects of its variations. Surely, the variable rated as least important — perhaps because it varied less frequently than the others — may be just as strategic as any of those with higher importance ratings. What we really need to know, however, is not the *comparative* importance of several factors but rather the effects of variations of each factor separately while the others remain unchanged.

If I want to know by how much an increase in the price of spinach may affect its consumption in an individual household, I shall not get very far by asking the householders to give a percentage rating to each of several listed factors that are believed to be "important" influences on spinach consumption. If it were tried, we should not be surprised to find changes in family income, the number of children and guests at dinner, and the notoriety of Popeye the Sailor's gusto for spinach, receiving much higher percentage ratings than changes in the price of spinach. (In a number of households price may not be a factor at all.) Nobody, I hope, would conclude from such a poll that price is an unimportant factor in the consumption of spinach.

Yet Professor Lester followed just this procedure when he wanted to find out how important wage rates were in determining the volume of employment in the individual firm. He asked the executives of the companies to "rate" the following factors "in terms of the percentage of importance of each":

a. Present and prospective market demand (sales for your products, including seasonal fluctuations in demand).
b. The level of wage rates or changes in the level of wages.
c. The level of material costs and other non-wage costs and changes in the level of such non-labor costs.

[14] R. A. Lester, *Am. Econ. Rev.,* Vol. XXXVI, No. 1, pp. 64–65.

d. Variations in profits or losses of the firm.
e. New techniques, equipment, and production methods.
f. Other factors (please specify).

Of these items the first unquestionably excels all others in frequency and extent of variations. That it won first prize in Professor Lester's importance contest is therefore not surprising. If several respondents gave ratings to item d (variations in profits or losses) and at the same time also to other items, they obviously did not realize that this variable comprised all the others. Professor Lester does not explain why he listed it when he knew that it was not "completely independent" and that "for example, wages affect profits."[15] Nor does he state whether the 43 firms which failed to mention changes in wage rates as an important factor meant that they would continue in business and continue to employ the same number of workers regardless of any degree of wage increase. If this is what they meant, they can hardly be taken seriously. If they meant something else, then it is not clear just what the replies should indicate about the probable effects of wage increases upon employment.

The strangest thing about Professor Lester's list of possibly important variables is that all — except f, the unspecified, and d, the all-inclusive profit-and-loss item — are essential variables of the very analysis which he means to disprove. The prize-winning item, a, the demand for the product, is certainly a most crucial determinant of marginal productivity. Items c, non-labor cost, and e, production techniques, are two other determinants of marginal productivity. How Professor Lester came to think that the results of this poll would in any sense disprove or shake marginal productivity analysis remains a mystery.

Questionnaire on Variable Cost

Professor Lester asked his business men also some questions on unit variable costs and profits at various rates of output. The information obtained in answer to these questions might have been useful had it not been based on an undefined concept of "plant capacity." Unfortunately, it must be suspected that not all firms meant the same thing when they referred to "100 per cent of capacity."

Economic theorists use different definitions of capacity. One widely-used definition marks as 100 per cent of capacity that volume of output at which short-run total cost per unit is a minimum; an-

---

[15] *Ibid.*, p. 66.

other definition fixes the 100 per cent mark at the output at which variable cost per unit is a minimum. The former definition implies decreasing average total cost, the latter decreasing average variable cost, up to "100 per cent capacity." Professor Lester after painstaking empirical research arrives at the following finding:

> The significant conclusion from the data in this section is that most of the manufacturing firms in the industries covered by this survey apparently have decreasing unit variable costs within the range of 70 to 100 per cent of capacity production. . . .[16]

Has Professor Lester asked himself whether this is not merely a self-evident conclusion implied in the definition of capacity used by his respondents?

The steepness of the reported decline in unit variable cost, however, would be an interesting observation — if the data were reliable. (Few of Professor Lester's firms had "constant unit variable costs," or anything approaching this situation, over a considerable range of output.) It is rather peculiar that unit variable costs should decrease steeply (at an increasing rate!) down to a certain point and then abruptly start rising — as one must infer from the term "100 per cent capacity." Where equipment is not utilized for 24 hours a day, the steep decline and abrupt rise of the unit cost is somewhat questionable.

Professor Lester, nevertheless, has sufficient confidence in his findings to draw conclusions — conclusions, moreover, which could not even be supported if the findings were of unquestionable validity. He states:

> If company output and employment policies are based on the assumption of decreasing marginal variable cost up to full capacity operations, much of the economic reasoning on company employment adjustments to increases and decreases in wage rates is invalid, and a new theory of wage-employment relationships for the individual firm must be developed.[17]

This deduction simply does not follow from the premises. There is no reason why decreasing marginal costs should invalidate the conventional propositions on factor cost and input. Professor Lester could have found dozens of textbook examples demonstrating the firm's reactions under conditions of decreasing marginal cost.

Professor Lester may have been deluded by a rather common confusion between related concepts: from decreasing marginal cost he may have jumped to the assumption of increasing labor returns, and from increasing physical returns he may have jumped to the

16 *Ibid.*, p. 71.
17 *Ibid.*, p. 71.

assumption of increasing marginal productivity of labor. Both these jumps are serious mistakes. For instance, the very conditions which may cause a firm to restrict the employment of labor to a volume still within the phase of increasing physical productivity per unit of labor are likely to result in decreasing marginal net revenue productivity of labor. These conditions are:

(a) an indivisibility of the firm's physical plant facilities,[18] combined with either (or both),

(b) a low elasticity of the demand for the firm's products[19] or (and)

(c) a low elasticity of the supply of labor to the firm.[20]

The first condition, (a), makes a phase of increasing physical productivity of labor in the firm a practical possibility; the other conditions, (b) or (c), make that phase relevant for actual operations by providing the pecuniary incentive to operate the plant inefficiently. Condition (b), the low elasticity of demand for the product, will cause marginal net revenue productivity of labor to be diminishing in a range of employment in which average or even marginal physical productivity of labor are still increasing.

It is not possible from Professor Lester's exposition to find out whether his failure to see these relationships was at the bottom of his faulty theorizing on this point. In any event, his findings on variable costs contain nothing that would even vaguely bear on the validity of marginal analysis.

Questionnaire on Adjustments

Professor Lester's fact-finding and theorizing on substitution between labor and capital and on other adjustments of the firm to changes in wage rates are also marred by inconsistencies and misunderstandings.

After trying to make the most of increasing returns to labor and only a few lines after referring to "unused plant capacity," Professor Lester asserts that "most industrial plants are designed and equipped for a certain output, requiring a certain work force. Often effective operation of the plant involves a work force of a given size."[21] To

---

[18] *I.e.*, the firm cannot adjust the number of machines or production units to smaller production volumes but must instead produce small outputs with an inefficiently large productive apparatus.

[19] *I.e.*, the firm realizes that it can charge much higher prices for smaller outputs or cannot dispose of larger outputs except with substantial price reductions.

[20] *I.e.*, the firm realizes that it can enjoy much lower wage rates at lower employment levels or cannot obtain more labor except with substantial wage increases.

[21] *Amer. Econ. Rev.*, Vol. XXXVI, No. 1, p. 72.

operate within the phase of increasing returns is to operate inefficiently, that is, with an employment of less labor with a given plant
than would be compatible with efficient operations. (Because an increase in employment would raise output more than proportionately.)
"Effective operation," on the other hand, logically implies employment at or beyond the point where diminishing returns set in. Professor Lester does not seem to be clear which way he wants to argue.[22]

Professor Lester seems to think that substitution between capital
and labor can occur only in the form of installation of new or scrap-
ping of existing machinery and that it is supposed to occur "readily"
and would, therefore, be "timed" with the wage changes. These are
rather common but nevertheless mistaken views.

Professor Lester does not discuss a glaring contradiction in his
findings: On the basis of replies to one questionnaire he states that
his data indicate "that industry does not adapt its plant and processes
to varying wage rates in the manner assumed by marginalists."
But on the basis of another questionnaire about adjustments to increases in relative wages, he reports that the introduction of "labor-
saving machinery" was given the highest rating in relative importance by the questioned firms whose labor costs were more than 29
per cent of total cost.

The last-mentioned questionnaire apparently was designed to
show that wage increases had no important effects upon employment.
Six alternative adjustments to increases in relative wages were listed
and manufacturers had to give percentage ratings for relative importance. In this popularity contest an item called "deliberate curtailment of output" got the booby prize. Quite apart from the fact that
the words were loaded against this item, the result is not in the least
surprising. For it is a well-known fact that where competition is not
pure (as it rarely is in industrial products), output adjustments to
higher production costs take place by way of changes in selling price.
Price and product adjustments were another of the alternative items
and scored rather well in the poll. If all employment-reducing adjustments — labor-saving machinery, price increases, and deliberate output curtailment — are taken together, they clearly dominate in the
importance ratings by the firms. This, or anything else, may not
mean much in such an "opinion poll," but it certainly does not prove
what Professor Lester wanted to prove. Nevertheless, he contends

[22] Absolutely fixed proportions between factors of production would imply
that short-run marginal productivity of labor drops precipitously to zero at the
full capacity level of employment.

that "it is especially noteworthy that deliberate curtailment of output, an adjustment stressed by conventional marginal theory, is mentioned by only four of the 43 firms." And he concludes that marginal analysis is all but done for, that "there can be little doubt about the correctness of the general results" of his tests, and that "a new direction for investigations of employment relationships and equilibrating adjustments in individual firms" is indicated.

C. Conclusions

I conclude that the marginal theory of business conduct of the firm has not been shaken, discredited or disproved by the empirical tests discussed in this paper. I conclude, furthermore, that empirical research on business policies cannot assure useful results if it employs the method of mailed questionnaires, if it is confined to direct questions without carefully devised checks, and if it aims at testing too broad and formal principles rather than more narrowly defined hypotheses.

The critical tone of my comments on the research projects discussed in this paper may give the impression of a hostile attitude towards empirical research as such. I wish to guard against such an impression. There should be no doubt that empirical research on the economics of the single firm is badly needed, no less than in many other fields. The correctness, applicability and relevance of economic theory constantly need testing through empirical research; such research may yield results of great significance.

Sharp criticism of bad research can be constructive in two respects: it may save some of the waste of time which the published research findings are apt to cause if they remain undisputed and are allowed to confuse hosts of students of economics; and it may contribute to the improvement of research. The chief condition for improved research is a thorough understanding of the theories to be tested. Supplementary conditions are a certain degree of familiarity with the technological and institutional peculiarities of the fields or cases on which the research is undertaken and a grasp of the research techniques employed.

COMMENT

Just because Machlup can point out weaknesses in Lester's questionnaire approach and in some of his conclusions does not mean that businessmen necessarily follow marginal principles. Similarly, just because businessmen could have acted marginally even though they did not understand marginalism and could not measure the relevant quantities does not mean they did so.

Two points raised in the papers greatly weaken the marginalist position. The first deals with the issue of non-pecuniary motives, the second with indivisibilities and inflexibility in the factors of production.

Machlup admits that businessmen have non-pecuniary goals in their decisions. To the extent that they do, the application of marginalism suffers. Machlup relegates these motives to scattered "exceptions and qualifications in the explanation of typical business conduct." Unfortunately for the marginalist case, we have only his opinion on this matter.

Apart from businessmen, workers themselves have non-pecuniary goals in their wage behavior. Satisfaction in the job, pleasant working conditions, etc., sometimes lead workers to accept wages below their marginal value product. There is even support for the power-forces school in at least one of the worker non-pecuniary, non-marginalist, motives. Seniority provisions in contracts reduce the importance of wages to the worker.

As for the indivisibility and lack of substitutability of factors, it should be recalled that almost all the respondents to Lester's questionnaire said they would not react to a wage increase by substituting machines for workers. Marginal productivity theorists could argue that the answers merely indicated indivisibilities in capital equipment, but the theory becomes valueless as an explanation of behavior if it merely states that employers would substitute if it were economical to do so, but admits that it seldom is.

Collective bargaining agreements often contain provisions which reduce the substitutability of productive factors. Controlling the speed or introduction of new machines reduces the ability to substitute machines for workers in response to wage increases. Provisions for dismissal or lay-off pay widens the range within which wages may increase before it would be economical to substitute machines for workers. These impediments to substitution related to collective bargaining, when added to inherent factor rigidity, greatly reduce the employment reducing adjustments demanded by strict adherence to marginal theory.

There is much more evidence against the application of marginalism than presented in Lester's study. The theory cannot explain the prevalence of differential wages for workers in the same labor market. According to the theory, intra-occupational differentials could exist only because of differences in efficiency but there is no evidence of these differences among workers. Overall regional wage differences could be explained because of the presence of relatively more labor than capital in the South compared with the North, but regional differences in the same industry using the same production methods cannot be explained on these grounds. Ignorance of wage levels elsewhere and labor immobility might account for the intra-occupational and regional differences but these are not marginal concepts. If marginalism applied, differential wage movements among industries should reflect differential productivity changes. It is this concept which the following paper treats, and fortunately for the harried marginalists, it reports just such corresponding movements.

JOHN T. DUNLOP

Productivity and the Wage Structure*

According to marginal productivity theory, an increase in productivity exerts downward pressure on prices and upward pressure on wages. If in a group of industries experiencing differential growth in productivity only the former pressure were effective, wage levels and wage structure would remain unchanged while individual industry prices would fall in correspondence to the productivity changes. On the other hand, if only wages moved in adjustment to the productivity changes, product prices would remain unchanged, and the move-

* Reprinted from *Income, Employment and Public Policy: Essays in Honor of Alvin H. Hansen*. By permission of W. W. Norton and Company, Inc. Copyright 1948 by W. W. Norton and Company, Inc.

ment of wages and productivity among the industries would correlate closely.

Dunlop rejects both of these possibilities as being too extreme, but suggests that both wage and price pressures will be felt so that, if marginal theory applies, there should occur more than average wage increases among those industries with more than average productivity gains and less than average increases in industries with less than average productivity gains. He then proceeds to test this variant of the marginal theory by calculating a correlation coefficient between wage and productivity movements. If his model approximates the actual adjustment that takes place, then of course the correlation cannot be perfect even if marginalism were rigidly applied because his study includes only two of the variables, productivity and wages; the price variable is not considered.

Dunlop cites other reasons for the absence of perfect correlation between the two variables—the need for preservation of traditional wage differences, different methods of wage payments (price and time)—varying degrees of competition in the product market, and differences in bargaining power. More will be said about this last, which Dunlop later relegates to an insignificant role, in the section on unionism. But as for the other three factors, they would each reflect their influence in differential price movements. Industries with relatively low productivity might experience greater wage increases than industries with high productivity growth if they tried to follow a policy of maintaining their relative wage position, if they paid by the piece, and if they operated on a monopolistic product market. The pattern of wage adjustment would be consistent with marginalism if the low productivity gains showed relatively high price increases. Presumably then, Dunlop would have expected marginal theory to be supported more closely if his data had permitted inclusion of relative price movements in the productivity study.

In any case, Dunlop found a relatively significant rank correlation between wage and physical productivity changes for a large number of industries over a relatively long period. The reader is left with an impression of the powerful influence of marginal factors. Not satisfied that the correlation between productivity and wage movements is significant, Dunlop continually stresses that this degree of relationship was achieved despite the presence of many forces tending to weaken the link between the two variables.

THE *levels* of prices and wage rates could vary over time under the impetus of increasing productivity in accordance with at least three logically possible patterns: (1) constant prices and rising wages, (2) falling prices and constant wages, and (3) rising prices with wages rising at an even faster pace. The actual movements of wage and price levels would appear more closely to approximate case (1) than either of the other two cases. The benefits of higher productivity have been shared since the early nineteenth century primarily by a combination of lower prices (for the innovations) and higher wage and salary rates.[1]

There is wide support for the view, moreover, that the general level of wage rates *should* as a matter of public policy rise in accordance with gains in productivity with a relatively constant price level. Professor Hansen concludes that ". . . there are good grounds for believing that the *long-run* movement of wages and prices broadly experienced in the nineteenth century represents the most desirable pattern."[2] The report of the Delegation on Economic Depressions admonishes trade union leaders that they should ". . . adopt a national wage policy under which demands for wage increases will be directly related to increases in productivity . . ."[3] The British White Paper on employment policy states that stability requires that ". . . increases in the general level of wage rates must be related to increased productivity due to increased efficiency and effort."[4]

The relative movements of wage and price levels in the next generation have been dramatized as a contest between the power of labor organizations to push up wage and salary rates on the one hand and the ability of scientists, engineers, and business enterprises to reduce costs and keep prices down on the other. The unions may not be content in the future with a wage level which advances no faster than 2 per cent each year, roughly the past average increase in productivity. They may require and be able to secure wage increases of 3 or 5 or 10 per cent each year. If the business community reduces

---

[1] The gains of productivity have also taken the form of "new" products or changes in quality, serviceability, durability, and performance. The problem of the participation of profits in the gains of technical change is discussed briefly in note 10.

[2] *Economic Policy and Full Employment,* Whittlesey House, McGraw-Hill Book Company, Inc., 1947, p. 243. Reprinted by permission.

[3] *Economic Stability in the Postwar World,* Report of the Delegation on Economic Depressions, League of Nations, 1945, p. 210.

[4] *Employment Policy,* Cmd. 6527, pp. 18–19.

costs and introduces new commodities fast enough, prices and wages can move as they have in the past, case (1). If union pressure on wage rates is greater, a new relationship will be established, case (3).

While these issues of wage and price *levels* are fundamental, the impact of changes in productivity on the *structure* of wage rates and prices has too frequently been overlooked. Wage rates cannot be adjusted uniquely to increases in productivity in each occupation and plant and preserve for very long a balanced wage structure.[5] The rates of increase in productivity are markedly divergent among different firms and industries. Normal or practicable wage rate relationships would soon be distorted if wage rates were to be geared absolutely to increases in productivity. While the general level of wages may be adjusted to the average increase in productivity, in particular occupations, firms, and industries, the total adjustment normally takes the form of a combination of a wage and salary rate increase, a price (including product) adjustment, and in the short run an increase in profits.[6]

The present paper is directed toward examining some of the implications and problems that arise when it is recognized that wage and salary rates cannot be adjusted fully to productivity[7] changes in every particular occupation, plant, firm, and industry. The study is an exercise in the relationship of wages and prices; its focus is the impact of changes in productivity on wage rate structure. The con-

[5] A balanced wage structure exists where workers performing similar services receive similar rates of pay. Variations in wage rates are related to differences in skill, experience, training, and other similar factors. The term will be used only in connection with the wage structure of a firm.

[6] While the present paper is not primarily devoted to the total problem of the way in which productivity gains are shared, the share of profits requires brief attention. The long run trends of wages and salaries and prices (including quality factors) indicate that productivity gains have been shared in these forms. Profits were not included in the list of long run recipients since the rate of profits has apparently shown no long term trend.

Profits, in the sense of "excess profit" above interest and wages of management, are necessary in the short run to induce enterprises to make the innovations. Under a perfectly competitive system, these "excess profits" are eliminated in the long run as the gains of productivity are passed on in the form of wage increases and price declines (including quality changes). See Joseph A. Schumpeter, *Business Cycles,* 1939, I, pp. 72–109.

[7] The term "productivity" is used in this paper in the narrow sense of physical input-output relationships. When a statistical measure is implied, output per manhour is intended. The distinction between physical and value productivity must be borne in mind. See National Bureau of Economic Research, *Cost Behavior and Price Policy,* 1943, pp. 142–169.

cern is the longer run — rather than the cyclical — adaptation of wage rates to uneven rates of change in productivity among different industries.

I. THE INDIVIDUAL PLANT WAGE STRUCTURE

The problems of the total system have their analogue in the individual plant. The rate of increase in productivity is unequal as among departments and particular machines. The job classification wage structure of a particular plant, determined by job evaluation or by a bargained scale, would soon be completely distorted if the gains in productivity were to go entirely to workers on particular operations with the improved efficiency. In practice, the gains in productivity may be described as temporarily retained in a "common pool" out of which the enterprise is able to grant a general wage increase to all employees. This procedure is also necessitated by the fact that many gains in productivity, such as those arising from improved organization and flow of operations, cannot be immediately allocated to particular workers.

Even under an incentive or piece rate system of wage payment most agreements provide for a modification of the rate in the event there has been a *substantial* change in job content.[8] Piece workers cannot normally be prevented from capturing certain small gains in productivity arising from minor changes in methods and machinery, since changes must normally be "substantial" in order to alter the piece rate. Piece rate earnings will consequently tend to show some upward drift relative to day-rated jobs. The war period produced a number of cases in which piece workers were able to capture very substantial increases arising from specific improvements in productivity. However, most of the larger gains in productivity are normally distributed more generally throughout the work force in a plant.

It is thus an established norm of collective bargaining within individual bargaining units that gains of productivity ought to be distributed in ways which will not indiscriminately distort the bal-

---

[8] As one example, the Carnegie-Illinois Steel Corporation's Contract with the United Steelworkers of America, March 13, 1945 in Section 4, F, 2, specifies the conditions under which new wage rates may be set for changed jobs:

"When changes are made in equipment, method of processing, material processed, or quality of production standards which would result in a substantial change in job duties or requirements; or where over a period of time an accumulation of minor changes of this type have occurred which, in total, have resulted in a substantial change in job duties or requirements, adjustments of hourly, incentive, piece-work and tonnage rates, may be required."

anced relationships among rates. Unequal rates of technical change may, however, in time substantially alter job relationships. In the garment industry, for example, over a number of years, as the result of a series of minor technical changes, the position of the presser (paid by the piece) has been improved relatively to the cutter (paid by the hour) so that he now earns more per hour on the average. But such an adjustment has come about slowly and quite gradually.

The extent of the bargaining unit will largely determine the group of job classifications among which differentials will be maintained or adjusted according to systematic principle with differential rates of increase in productivity. If the bargaining unit is plant wide, the whole structure of rates in the plant will be less subject to productivity distortions. If there should be several bargaining units, the plant structure of rates will be much more difficult for the company to systematize and to defend against unequal rates of technical change.

As bargaining units are extended to multi-plant companies and to a group of companies or an industry, the agreed-upon structure of differentials is less subject to the haphazard impact of differential increases in productivity. Since few, if any, bargaining units completely encompass more than one industry, industry differentials have not been the result of conscious, intended decisions.

Thus two factors, the method of wage payment and the extent of the bargaining unit, will substantially influence the impact of changes in productivity on the structure of job classification wage rates in the individual plant.

II. PRODUCTIVITY AND INTER-INDUSTRY WAGE CHANGES

Consider the general level of wage rates for the system as a whole to increase each period by the average amount of the increase in productivity in the system. The rates of increase in productivity vary widely among industries and firms. (a) At one extreme, it might be assumed that the wage rate adjustments in each firm and industry correspond to these different increases in productivity. Normal wage relationships would be completely distorted. (b) At the other extreme, it might be assumed that the wage structure was so inflexible that there could be no change in firm or industry differentials. Wage rates would rise in every firm by the same amount. Then in industries in which productivity increased less rapidly than the average, prices would rise, and in industries in which productivity increased more rapidly than the average, prices would fall.

In the first case (a), the effect of the different rates of increase (or decrease in a few cases) of productivity is absorbed entirely through diverse wage and salary rate changes. In the second case (b), the divergent productivity patterns result alone in price adjustments. The wage structure, however, is in fact neither so flexible as assumed in the first instance nor so inflexible as imagined in the second.

A more realistic model, case (c), depicts industries with *more* than average gains in productivity increasing wage and salary rates somewhat more than the average. In industries with *less* than average gains in productivity, wage rates would increase somewhat less than average.

The rates of increase in productivity in an industry are to be expected to be closely related to other characteristics of the industry. The growth in output and employment[9] of various industries is frequently said to chart a common pattern. A period of slow growth at the initial stages is followed by a rapid expansion; a tapering off develops which may be followed in some cases by actual contraction and even extinction of the industry. The most rapid increases in productivity are to be expected in those stages in the life history of an industry during which output is expanding rapidly. Increases in productivity do take place after output has begun to taper off, but the opportunities for innovations of all types would seem on *a priori* grounds less favorable when output had ceased to expand or was actually decreasing.

The model of the relation between wage rate changes and productivity increments, case (c) above, needs to be enlarged, then, to take account of this kinship between changes in productivity and output. The greater than average rise in wage and salary rates in industries with high rates of increase in productivity arises not merely because firms may be able to pay higher wages or may be unable to prevent employees from taking some of the benefits. The greater than average rise in wage rates will be necessary to attract an expanding work force to the industry. The labor market typically operates so that a relatively higher wage rate is necessary to attract wage earners away from other employment than is required to hold them at a given job. Normal inertia must be overcome. Seniority rights are not lightly forfeited. A large proportion of all jobs are filled through contacts established by friends and relatives. These factors require that

---

[9] The patterns of movement will, of course, be different depending on the rates of change in productivity.

any firm or industry which seeks to expand its employment rapidly must expect to pay a premium rate.

Thus the greater than average rise of wage rates in employment and productivity expanding industries tends to attract a labor force to such industries. Similarly, the less than average increase in wage rates in employment and productivity contracting industries tends to facilitate the movement of a labor force away from such industries and to deter new entrants.

Moreover, the rise in prices in industries in which the increase in productivity is less than the average tends to accelerate the relative or absolute contraction of employment in such industries. The failure of prices to fall in industries with greater than average increases in productivity, as far as they might otherwise, tends to restrict the expansion of employment from what it would otherwise be. These relatively adverse effects on employment constitute the short-run effects of movement toward the longer run equilibrium position in which the average wage level is adjusted to an increase in average productivity.

Professor Hansen has suggested that the model, case (c), of the relationship between wage and salary rates, employment and productivity, is in fact a fair description of the actual world.[10] The next section turns to an examination of the available statistical data.

III. THE STATISTICAL EVIDENCE

There is considerable evidence that productivity has increased most in industries in which employment has expanded most, and there is some evidence that productivity has increased most rapidly during the "life-cycle" of an industry when employment was expanding most rapidly. Productivity conversely seems to have increased least in

[10] "If industry Y can make no gains in productivity, it will nevertheless be compelled to pay higher wages. Being a relatively stagnant industry, it would scarcely be expected to raise wages as soon, or even as far, as the progressive industries. But wages must go up, or else a violent distortion will occur in the wage structure. Since industry Y has enjoyed no gains in manhour productivity, it must be permitted to charge higher prices.

"Thus the exceptionally progressive industries will be able to *lower* prices. But the stagnant industries will need to raise prices. Industries enjoying *average* gains in productivity can raise wages without raising prices. The net effect is an all-round increase in wage rates, while the general level of prices remains stable. But while the *general level* of prices remains stable, the *structure* of prices is changing in accordance with changing technological conditions varying from industry to industry." Alvin H. Hansen, "Wages and Prices: The Basic Issue," *New York Times Magazine*, January 6, 1946. Reprinted by permission.

industries with the least increase, or actual declines, in employment, or in those stages in the life of an industry in which employment has been declining.

On the basis of data for thirty-eight manufacturing industries covering the period 1909–37 Solomon Fabricant reports that ". . . exceptionally rapid growth in output was associated with unusually drastic cuts in manhours per unit. Slow growth or actual decline in output was accompanied by less-than-average increase in total manhours and by relatively small declines in the manhour-output ratio."[11] Data for the same industries support the further conclusion that industries with the most rapid increase in employment and output and with the greatest rate of increase in productivity were also those with ". . . lowest increases (or actual decreases) in wage cost per unit, value added per unit, and selling price."[12] The converse holds for industries laggard in output, employment, and productivity.

Thus the Fabricant study depicts an economy with a group of "younger" industries expanding rapidly in employment, output, and productivity with declining labor costs and prices. In a group of "older" industries employment and output increase very slowly or actually decline; productivity increases very slowly, and labor costs and prices increase absolutely, or at least relative to the first group of industries. The life history of the individual industry consists in a gradual movement from the first to the second group. At any one time industries are distributed throughout the range of the employment-output-productivity pattern.

Now, how are wage rate movements among industries related to the pattern of change in output, employment, and productivity? In particular, do wage rates increase most where and when productivity is increasing most rapidly, and do wage rates increase least in industries with least increases in productivity? The intermediate case (c) set forth above requires some positive correlation between increases in wage rates and productivity. Professor Hansen, it has been noted, believes both that the economy should and really does work this way.

While the investigation of Solomon Fabricant was not primarily concerned with this range of questions, there is some disquieting

---

[11] Solomon Fabricant, *Employment in Manufacturing, 1899–1939,* National Bureau of Economic Research, 1942, p. 92. Reprinted by permission. Also see, Solomon Fabricant, *Labor Savings in American Industry, 1899–1939,* Occasional Paper 23, National Bureau of Economic Research, 1945.

[12] Solomon Fabricant, *Employment in Manufacturing, op. cit.,* p. 100.

evidence on the issue at hand. He reports that the coefficient of rank correlation ". . . between changes in unit labor requirements and in wages per worker is only — .05."[13] That is, for the period 1909–37 virtually no rank correlation was found in a group of thirty-eight industries between changes in productivity (wage earner hours per unit of product) and *wages per wage earner*.

Although Fabricant does not report the computation, his data permit a comparison of productivity (wage earner hours per unit of product) and *wages per hour*. The rank correlation has been computed to be +.22. The series of wages per hour is more appropriate for the instant purposes than wages per worker. Wages per worker are affected by varying rates of change in the length of the work day.

More reliable data for a shorter, though more recent, period show a much higher degree of rank correlation between productivity increases and wages. The Bureau of Labor Statistics data for thirty-three manufacturing industries or groups in the period 1923–40 yield a rank correlation of +.47 between increases in output per manhour and increases in average hourly earnings.[14] (These data are presented in Table I.) When the series are weighted by the relative amounts of employment in the various industries, the rank correlation is raised to +.60.

The removal of two relatively insignificant industries from the series (ice cream and chewing tobacco) raises the computed rank correlation to +.65. When the series are weighted by employment in the various industries, the rank correlation is +.72. These data indicate a significant tendency, not necessarily unique, for wages to increase by a greater extent in industries with the higher increases in productivity and by a lesser extent in industries with lesser increases in productivity.

The relationship between wages and productivity proposed in

13 *Loc. cit.*, p. 105, n. 19. The computation has been made for the present study on the basis of data presented on pp. 102–104 and the slightly different result of +.04 was obtained.

14 The basic data are from *Productivity and Unit Labor Costs in Selected Manufacturing Industries, 1919–1940,* Bureau of Labor Statistics, Washington, D. C., February, 1942. The output per manhour series is directly available, and the series of average hourly earnings for each industry was computed by dividing payrolls by manhours. The data are available to permit the addition of a series for Bituminous Coal and Steam Railroads. The rank correlation for the thirty-five series is +.49.

Average hourly earnings are the only data available to measure the changes in wage and salary rates for this period.

case (c) in the previous section does not posit a unique pattern nor necessarily a very high correlation between wages and salary rates and productivity. The following factors act against a perfect correlation:

(1) The adjustment to productivity increases takes the form of price as well as wage changes. Thus one would expect a higher degree of correlation between changes in unit labor requirements and wages.[15]

(2) Wage relationships may have to be preserved among industries, regardless of the differences in the rates of increase of productivity. The wage relationship may follow from a common labor organization, the proximity of localities, or a common policy of a corporation operating in several industries. The cotton and wool industries, for example, are organized by some of the same labor organizations. Wage patterns may be related independently of productivity. Zinc and copper present the same situation. An "industry" is not necessarily a unique unit of wage rate determination.

(3) The method of wage payment may differ among industries and influence the extent to which increases in productivity are transformed into wage increases. Piece work or incentive rates permit a more regular and immediate capture of the gains of productivity than a day-rate wage payment system.

(4) The character of competition in the product market will influence the extent to which wage earners secure the gains of productivity. A highly competitive product market may immediately transmit any gains in productivity in the form of price adjustments rather than permit the employer to retain higher margins later to be shared with the wage earners in the form of higher wage rates. Partly for this reason, labor organization may prefer to deal with "monopolists" rather than with a "competitive industry." It is easier to capture the dynamic gains of productivity.

(5) The differences in bargaining power of labor organizations will influence the extent to which gains in productivity will be correlated with wage rate changes.

For at least these reasons, then, wage rate changes and increases in productivity are not uniquely related among different firms and industries. There is no reason, however, to abandon the general model indicated in case (c) above in which wage rates increase most

---

[15] Fabricant reports a .39 rank correlation between changes in unit labor requirements and selling price in contrast to his −.05 rank correlation between changes in unit labor requirements and wages. *Loc. cit.*, p. 108.

TABLE I — PERCENTAGE CHANGE IN OUTPUT, MANHOURS, OUTPUT PER
MANHOUR, AND AVERAGE HOURLY EARNINGS, 1923–1940*

Industry	Change in output	Change in manhours	Change in output per manhour	Change in av. hourly earnings
	%	%	%	%
All manufacturing industries	52.5	−16.6	82.9	22.5
Agricultural implements	54.4	−26.2	109.4	33.5
Boots and shoes	18.4	−28.9	66.7	−3.7
Bread and other bakery products group	29.8	15.4	12.4	19.6
Cane-sugar refining	−4.5	−38.4	54.9	32.6
Canning and preserving group	82.9	7.3	70.5	28.6
Cement	−4.5	−46.3	78.1	25.7
Chemicals	103.2	−0.5	104.3	64.1
Clay products and non-clay refractories	−42.1	−52.0	20.5	6.1
Cotton goods, New England states	−49.2	−71.7	79.4	3.3
Cotton goods, cotton-growing states	45.5	18.5	22.7	13.0
Fertilizers	17.2	−25.2	56.7	20.9
Flour and other grain mill products	−12.6	−41.9	50.7	15.8
Furniture	15.4	−18.9	42.4	3.1
Glass group	67.4	−22.0	114.5	42.7
Ice cream	36.1	−44.3	144.5	−1.4
Iron and steel group	41.2	−22.6	82.5	45.5
Knit goods group	72.2	−7.7	86.7	29.5
Leather group	−6.3	−41.7	61.3	25.8
Lumber and timber products group	−24.2	−49.1	49.0	10.7
Motor vehicles, bodies, and parts	44.0	−16.5	72.5	36.5
Newspaper and periodical ptg. & pub.	36.5	−17.2	64.9	25.3
Primary smelters and refineries	23.4	−29.3	74.3	14.5
Paints and varnishes	57.5	2.8	53.3	37.2
Paper	68.8	5.9	59.4	22.2
Pulp	148.4	−8.4	171.3	35.8
Petroleum refining	128.7	−18.3	180.1	53.4
Rayon	1177.7	162.7	386.4	56.4
Rubber tires and inner tubes	105.0	−39.9	241.0	44.6
Slaughtering and meat packing	17.7	−14.3	37.3	26.8
Cigars	−27.0	−66.7	119.0	17.0
Cigarettes	183.9	19.3	138.0	40.0
Chewing and smoking tobacco and snuff	−16.5	−46.4	55.7	69.2
Woolen and worsted goods group	−22.3	−46.8	45.9	22.0
Bituminous coal	−18.4	−10.2	42.3	4.5
Steam railroads	....	−3.1	63.2	22.4

* The figures in this table are based on Bureau of Labor Statistics indexes and indicate
percentage changes for the years 1923–1940, with the exception of the following industries where the percentage changes are for the years 1923–1939:

Cotton Goods: New England States
Cotton Goods: Cotton Growing States
Knit Goods Group

in those industries in which employment, output, and productivity have increased most rapidly, and in which wage rates increase least in those industries in which employment, output, and productivity have increased least rapidly — if not actually declined. The model is a helpful and useful generalization and first approximation, particularly for total system problems, as long as the other factors influencing wage rate movements among industries are not entirely neglected. Professor Hansen's adoption of the model as a statement of fact is accurate as long as productivity is not set forth as a complete explanation of change in inter-industry wage structure.

IV. WAGE LEADERSHIP

Any model of adjustments in the wage structure cannot neglect the facts of wage leadership in an economy with developing collective bargaining. If leadership in setting the pattern of wage adjustments is held by unions and firms in the expanding sector, where increases in productivity are high, the rounds of wage increases will no doubt be larger than in case the pace is set in contracting industries. Even among expanding industries it makes a good deal of difference whether the two or three most rapidly expanding industries set the pace or whether the pattern is more broadly based. It is conceivable that the wage bargain in one or two industries (rapidly expanding with the greatest increases in productivity) could force very substantial price increases on the rest of the whole economy.

It may be held that in normal times "wage leadership" does not exist. There is no very obvious pattern of wage changes. Contracts expire at different times, and adjustments depend upon essentially local or industry conditions. The amount of wage rate changes are substantially influenced by bargains over non-wage issues, such as union security, seniority, and management rights clauses in collective bargaining contracts. While this may be a fair description of the situation in the absence of powerful unions or in conditions in which significant union rivalry does not exist, it is not an accurate description of the industrial relations we have now or are likely to have in the years immediately ahead.

The location of wage leadership in the economic system depends on a great many different factors. With a united labor movement there would presumably be a possibility of a common wage policy on the part of organized labor. Intense inter- and intra-union rivalry, however, tends to make wage movements a pawn in the larger battle for prestige and position. Wage changes may be required sooner and in larger amounts by virtue of the strategy of these union "political" considerations. Wage demands are not formulated with primary regard to their economic effects. A wage adjustment is largely appraised in terms of how many new members may be attracted or whether it will contribute to "taking over" a rival organization.

An organized employers' association which influences wage bargaining would permit a unified policy on the part of employers. In the absence of strong associations in most industries, wage rate patterns may be set by a maverick company which wishes to purchase some temporary advantage, or by an extraordinarily profitable enterprise which may not be particularly interested or concerned with the general impact of any change in wage rates. The business community is learning that one or two major companies can make a bargain which becomes very difficult for the rest to avoid.

Wage leadership may be located in particular industries by virtue of the "political" position of union leaders within the labor movement, by the accidents of mavericks and extraordinarily profitable firms, and by the chance of the timing of contract expirations. If this leadership happens to coincide with industries in which productivity has been increasing rapidly, the wage level may be expected to rise more than in other circumstances.

V. CHANGES IN INTER-INDUSTRY WAGE STRUCTURE

The model investigated above, case (c), seems to represent a useful general summary of the relations among inter-industry changes in productivity, employment, and wage and salary rates. But this generalization, even when qualified by the fact of wage leadership in collective bargaining, must not be taken as a final theory of the dynamics of changes in inter-industry wage relationships. This section is directed toward making some suggestions toward this larger and virtually unexplored problem of the pattern of longer run changes in the inter-industry wage structure.

That the generalization represented by case (c) is a useful starting point for a theory of the dynamics of inter-industry wage changes is evident from Table II.[16] An array of the percentage changes in average hourly earnings during the period 1923–40 is presented for thirty-three manufacturing industries (with the addition of two other series, Bituminous Coal and Steam Railroads). The lowest fourteen industrial groups in percentage increase in average hourly

[16] The data are the same as presented in Table I.

earnings (Woolen and Worsted through Boots and Shoes) were almost without exception[17] industries with productivity and output increases below the average. The highest twelve industrial groups in percentage increase in average hourly earnings (Chewing Tobacco through Agricultural Implements) were with minor exceptions[18] industries with productivity and output increases above the average. The mere recital of the industries with the greatest increase in average hourly earnings suggests those expanding in output and progressive in technology: Chemicals, Rayon, Petroleum Refining, Iron and Steel, Rubber Tires and Tubes, Glass, Cigarettes, Paints and Varnish, Motor Vehicles, Pulp, and Agricultural Implements.

A study of Table II underlines the severe limitations to the view that inter-industry wage differentials are relatively constant over considerable periods of time. These thirty-five industrial groups reveal during a seventeen-year period a dispersion from a decrease of 3.7 per cent in the case of Boots and Shoes to an increase of 64.1 per cent in Chemicals.[19] This range of variation constitutes a surprising amount of pliability in the inter-industry wage structure.

The dispersion in Table II casts serious doubts on the position frequently taken in favor of a wage increase in negotiations or arbitration on the ground that traditional inter-industry differentials have been distorted. The longer the period of comparison, the more suspect the argument. The argument advanced against wage rate increases by managements on the ground that inter-industry differentials have been maintained, and consequently no increase is appropriate, is equally suspect. Changes in the differentials in wages among industries of the magnitude indicated in Table II in a period of seventeen years makes such arguments highly questionable as a strong case for or against a particular wage rate increase. The simple fact is that the relative position of industries has been changing very rapidly over a period of time. Relative position cannot be a satisfactory norm for any significant length of time in an economy with such marked differences in the rate of change in employment and productivity.

[17] The series of Ice Cream and Cigars showed increases in output per man-hour above the average.

[18] Chewing Tobacco, at the top of the list, is an exception. In output and productivity the industry belongs with the relatively "stagnant" group. The industry has been omitted from later comparisons in the text.

[19] Any complete study of movement of differentials should be made both in percentage and cents per hour terms. The cents per hour differentials in these instances would not reveal a significantly different picture. Moreover, the period 1923–40 saw an increase in the average hourly earnings for all manufacturing of only 22.5 per cent.

TABLE II — PERCENTAGE INCREASE IN AVERAGE HOURLY EARNINGS, 1923–1940

Industry	Percentage increase in average hourly earnings
1. Chewing and smoking tobacco and snuff	69.2
2. Chemicals	64.1
3. Rayon	56.4
4. Petroleum refining	53.4
5. Iron and steel	45.5
6. Rubber tires and inner tubes	44.6
7. Glass	42.7
8. Cigarettes	40.0
9. Paints and varnishes	37.2
10. Motor vehicles, bodies, and parts	36.5
11. Pulp	35.8
12. Agricultural implements	33.5
13. Cane-sugar refining	32.6
14. Knit goods	29.5
15. Canning and preserving	28.6
16. Slaughtering and meat packing	26.8
17. Leather	25.8
18. Cement	25.7
19. Newspaper and periodical printing and publishing	25.3
20. Steam railroads (Class I)	22.4
21. Paper	22.2
22. Woolen and worsted goods	22.0
23. Fertilizers	20.9
24. Bread and other bakery products	19.6
25. Cigars	17.0
26. Flour and other grain mill products	15.8
27. Primary smelters and refineries	14.5
28. Cotton goods — cotton growing states	13.0
29. Lumber and timber products	10.7
30. Clay products and nonclay refractories	6.1
31. Bituminous coal	4.5
32. Cotton goods — New England states	3.3
33. Furniture	3.1
34. Ice cream	−1.4
35. Boots and shoes	−3.7

The dispersion in Table II suggests that a theory of the inter-industry movement of wage structure must include other factors than changes in productivity and output or employment. Three additional factors are suggested for consideration: the proportion of labor costs to total costs in the industry, the competitive conditions in the product market for the output of the industry, and the skill composition of the industry. While these factors may be in part directly related to changes in productivity and output, their separate influences on patterns of wage movement should be distinguished.

The smaller the proportion of labor costs to total outlays, other factors being the same, the more likely for wage and salary rates to rise relative to the average of all industries. Wage and salary earners will have greater bargaining power, and enterprises will tend to offer less resistance to increases.

The more competitive the product markets for the output of the industry, the more difficult for wage earners to capture the gains of increased productivity. The competitive conditions in the product markets for Boots and Shoes, Cotton Textiles, Bituminous Coal, and Furniture undoubtedly influenced the pattern of wage changes in these industries.

The skill composition of the industry, as it is altered through time by technological change, will affect seriously the pattern of movement in average hourly earnings. Two industries may have the same rate of increase in output per manhour, but the wage patterns will diverge because the average level of skill, or the occupational composition, of the work force in the industries will be changing in different directions.

The inter-industry pattern of changes in average hourly earnings over substantial periods is to be explained fundamentally in terms of the following factors: change in productivity, change in output, proportion of labor costs to total outlays, competitive conditions in the product market, and the changing skill and occupational content of the industry. Wage and salary rates would be expected to increase most where productivity and output increase most, where labor costs are a small percentage of total costs, where the enterprises are in strong bargaining power with the purchasers of their output, and where technical change operates to increase the skill and raise the occupational rating of employees. The converse indicates situations where wage and salary rates are to be expected to decline relatively.

This theoretical framework for inter-industry wage movements appears to give no distinctive place to the role of labor organizations. The discussion in the section on wage leadership indicated that labor organizations can have a decisive influence on the wage and salary level. Their influence on the structure of wages cannot be ignored. The data in Table II do not suggest that the role of unionization has been distinctive or uniform. A careful statement would suggest that the five factors indicated above establish the main outlines and tendencies for variations in inter-industry wage relationships. These factors are important realities (although not the full story) with which the parties to collective bargaining must grapple. They tend to set practicable limits to bargains. When account is taken of all the factors which must be taken into account by the parties to collective bargaining, the final wage bargain may diverge, even over long periods, from that indicated by the theoretical framework suggested above. While judgments will differ, the present observer is of the opinion that in most cases the divergence will not be large. The factors indicated in the theoretical model effectively condition the bargaining process.

VI. SUMMARY

It may be helpful to highlight the previous discussion by a series of propositions. These points must be interpreted within the context developed in previous sections.

(1) The benefits of higher productivity have been shared over long periods by a combination of lower prices and higher wage rates. There have also been significant changes in quality.

(2) Wage rates show some tendency to increase most in that group of industries in which output, employment, and productivity increase most. Wage rates increase least in those industries in which output, employment, and productivity increase least. This generalization is a useful and valid summary.

(3) The relationship between changes in productivity and wage rates, however, is not unique since a great many other factors affect wage-rate movements among industries.

(4) The location of wage leadership in the system, as between expanding and contracting sectors, can materially affect the rate of rise in the average wage level.

(5) The argument for or against an increase in wage rates in a particular industry or firm on the grounds of productivity would appear much less valid than normally assumed. The standard of productivity by which the parties are admonished to settle their disputes is an empty slogan as judged by the historical pattern of wage and productivity changes for any particular wage bargain.

(6) Wage differentials among industries appear to have been surprisingly flexible. In a seventeen-year period there have been marked changes in the relative position of wages in expanding and contracting industries.

(7) The argument that wages should be increased in an industry to preserve its relative position, or that they should not be increased

because wages in a particular industry are at parity with other industries is dangerous, for it neglects the highly dynamic character of wage differentials among industries.

(8) The inter-industry variations in wages over substantial periods are to be explained in terms of these factors: changes in productivity and output, the proportion of labor costs to total costs, the competitive conditions in the product market for the output of an industry, and the changing skill and occupational content of the work force of an industry. These factors will tend to set limits to the bargaining over the relative position of the wage and salary rates of the employees of an industry.

COMMENT

Dunlop bases his reasoning that factors other than productivity must have a strong influence on wages, and thus weaken the wage-productivity correlation, on the character of his Table II. The array of wage changes for the industry studies seems to him to show such wide dispersion as to imply that numerous and sometimes opposing forces must impinge on wages. However, if an array had been made of the productivity changes themselves, they would have described as wide a dispersion as the array of wages. Thus if it is only the width of the wage dispersion that causes concern, the equally strong variation in the hypothesized independent variable, productivity, would be adequate explanation for the wage spread.

Despite this argument against the relevance of Table II, it is worthwhile to review Dunlop's four other factors that might influence wages output, the ratio of labor cost to total cost, degree of competition in the product market, and changes in occupational content within industries to conclude whether or not they operate to reduce the relationship between wages and productivity.

Output, as Dunlop notes in his review of Fabricant's work, tends to be positively correlated with productivity. That is, expanding industries usually experience the most substantial productivity gains. Thus, the omission of the variable output creates no disruptive bias to the wage-productivity relationship. If anything it might lead to a high calculated correlation when no true relationship exists. For if we accept the hypothesis that expanding industries must pay high wages, then a high correlation between wages and productivity may really result from the close relationship between wages and output, with which productivity is correlated.

As for the importance to which Dunlop attributes the share of labor costs to total costs in influencing wages, there is a suggestion here of acceptance of a discredited Marshallian postulate of derived demand. The implication is that firms whose labor costs are but a small share of total costs will have an inelastic demand for labor and will be more inclined to pass on productivity gains to workers in the form of higher wages than firms whose labor costs are a large share of total costs and whose labor demand is elastic. Since there is no basis for assuming a relationship between productivity and the ratio of labor costs to total costs among industries, the two-variable wage-productivity correlation would be weakened were wages influenced by the labor-cost-ratio factor. But Marshall's position that relatively low labor costs necessarily lead to inelastic labor demand, implied in Dunlop's presentation, has since been disproved and the mathematical proof that a high labor cost-ratio creates a low labor demand elasticity only under special conditions has been incorporated in economic theory.

The degree of competition in the product market may influence wages; monopolistic industries may have a less elastic labor demand schedule than industries operating in competitive markets. To the extent that this occurs, the rank correlation between wages and productivity tends to be reduced if it is accepted that there is no relationship between the degree of monopoly and productivity changes among industries.

Dunlop's mention of the occupational content factor is an acknowledgment that the industry is a very diffuse unit for wage analysis. Many occupations are included, and average industry wages will change even though every one of its occupational wages remains unchanged because of the shift in the occupational mix as productive techniques are altered. Thus a change in an industry's average wage represents the combined effect of wage changes and occupational shifts. It might be argued that shifts in the occupational mix toward higher paying jobs go together with productivity changes, so that the wage-productivity correlation is not weakened by this shift. Therefore, although the wage-productivity comparison may no longer be the correct one for testing marginal influences, which refer to actual wage changes, at least the shift in the skill or occupational mix within industries is not a factor tending to reduce the wage-productivity correlation of the type of Dunlop's study.

In summary, then, the only factor other than productivity which Dunlop considers to influence wages that tends to reduce the wage-productivity relationship is the degree of competition in the product market. Nevertheless, the degree of relationship this study found between wage and productivity movements was significant. Unfortunately for the cause of marginalism other studies of a similar nature, using different data, did not find the same close relationship.

Consider the Fabricant study, cited by Dunlop. Even after Dunlop altered the correlation from between productivity changes and wages per worker to productivity changes and wages per hour, the rank correlation for the Fabricant industries was only $+22$. However, this study did show a very close inverse relationship between wage costs per unit of output and productivity; that is, those industries with the greater gains in productivity had the lower increases (even declines in some cases) in wages per unit of output. This result implied a tendency toward uniformity in wage changes, and differential pressures of labor cost on product prices. The industries with the smallest productivity gains tended to experience the greatest price pressures from changes in labor costs.

All this suggests a missing ingredient in the testing of the influence of marginal principles on wage movements. This element is the relative movement of product prices among the industries. According to marginal productivity theory, a gain in productivity can be distributed between price declines and wage increases. The Dunlop type of study, which only relates wages to productivity changes, leads to erratic results since price adjustments, consistent with marginalism, weaken the simple two-way wage-productivity comparison.

For example, industry A may show a greater productivity growth than industry B, but if the former industry undergoes a greater price adjustment (relative decline) than B, its wages may not rise as much. There will not then be a positive correlation between wages and productivity for the two industries, though marginal principles are followed.

Thus, to test the applicability of marginalism, the correct productivity variable is not physical productivity changes but value productivity changes. The value concept includes the price variable. Studies of the relationship between value productivity movements and wages have yielded high correlations between the two variables. This parallel movement indicates adjustment according to marginal principles. However, this does not necessarily mean that economic rather than power forces are more important wage determinants. The sequence need not run from productivity or product price changes to wage adjustments. The data could just as easily fit a pattern of adjustments that started from effective union wage pressure to price and productivity changes along marginal lines.

Although the adjustment might follow orthodox marginalism, the issue of whether economic or power forces are the prime wage movers remains unclarified. If the marginal productivity theory approach leaves this issue uncertain, the student of wages will find as high a degree of indecision in the direct approach which tries to appraise the extent of union influence on wages.

PART TWO

UNION INFLUENCE ON WAGES

INTRODUCTION
Statistical and Methodological Problems

From a statistical point of view, a major difficulty in evaluating the effect of unions on wages is the measurement of the unionism variable. Since the importance of union wage pressure, even by the strongest adherents of the power-forces school, is not considered to vary with small differences in the degree of unionization, studies usually relate wage levels or wage movements to situations in which the differences in degree of unionization are substantial. For example, to compare union with nonunion wages for a group of industries, the former category might include industries with, say, over 50 per cent unionization and the latter with, say, under 50 per cent. When this is done, statistical tests of significance of wage differences must not only allow for comparisons of average levels, but also of dispersion of rates within each category. Apart from the degree of statistical sophistication required by the reader to understand this analysis, there is the problem of the need for detailed wage data for all the industries, and firms within the industries.

As for methodological problems, without going into the measurement of the degree of influence, it is the aim of studies of the effect of unionism on wages to conclude whether or not the process of collective bargaining leads to higher wages. The usual technique is to compare union and nonunion wages in a particular setting. When wages are higher for the union than the nonunion workers, it might signify that unionism was responsible for the higher wage of the average unionized workers. However, the higher wages could have resulted from factors other than unionism.

Similarly, when statistical analysis reveals no difference between union and nonunion wages in a particular setting, this need not mean that unionism was not an active independent force for higher wages. In the nonunion sector, wages might have risen in response to the rise in union wages. Management might have raised wages to the union level perhaps to maintain worker morale, or more likely, to parry the threat of unionization.

Power force advocates are certain of carrying their point if they conclude that when union wages are higher than nonunion wages, unionism is responsible for the difference and that when the wages are equal the nonunion sector reacted to the indirect forces generated by union wage pressure. By the same token, the market-force supporters would always minimize the importance of union activity in the wage field if they concluded that the presence of a union-non-union wage differential could be explained on economic grounds and its absence proof that unionism was ineffective in raising wages. These possibilities seem to emphasize the need for caution in reaching conclusions regarding the effect of union wage activity from the mere presence or absence of a union-nonunion differential.

Selected Readings

Selections on "Union Influence on Wages" begin with Clark Kerr's summary paper, "Wage Relationships—The Comparative Impact of Market and Power Forces." Although its title includes the central terms of this entire collection, the paper really summarizes conclusions of the influence of unionism on wages. As a summary it is the least polemical of all the papers included, but at the same time its conclusions have the least statistical substantiation. It is included as an excellent guide both to the different approaches to the problem of appraising union wage influences, and to the scope of the subject. Kerr does not write of the relationship between union and nonunion wages in general but of the impact of unionism on specific wage structures, whether occupational, industrial, or interregional.

Arthur Ross' *Trade Union Wage Policy* is one of the most noted sources of the power-forces school. This book, a collection of earlier papers, takes the position that wages are determined by the power struggle at the bargaining table. A small excerpt from this book has been selected as an eloquent statement of the power-forces approach.

Ross' position is not simply that unions raise wages, as he attempts to demonstrate in the last chapter of his book, but, as appears in this excerpt, that union wage activity is complex and itself dominated by political considerations to the extent that the maximum wage is not always sought.

A large number of statistical studies have concluded that unions have raised wages. Some of these studies are on the interfirm or interindustry level. These studies attempt to isolate the influence of unionism from that of other factors. Of course the narrower the study, the more readily this can be accomplished. Ozanne's study is selected as an example of the heroic approach. It attempts to test the influence of unionism as such on the general level of industrial wages, and concludes that wages have been significantly higher during the current era of unionism than in earlier nonunion days, because of union wage activity.

While Ozanne's study is as broad as the manufacturing sector itself, Maher's "Union, Nonunion Wage Differentials," the last selection included, is a focused study of limited data. Painstaking effort is made to isolate the variable of unionism. His analysis leads Maher to the conclusion that wages are unaffected by unionism, at least for the data studied. Dunlop, it has been noted, inferred that unionism was unimportant in wage setting for the industries of his study because they followed a wage-productivity pattern consistent with marginalism; Maher reached the same conclusion by a direct comparison of union and nonunion wages. Maher makes no rash extrapolation from his limited study, but his work emphasizes the need for isolating the unionism factor in order to assign unionism as a cause for union-nonunion differential wage movements. Although most studies seem to show some union influence on wages, Maher's work is part of a small but important body of literature which presents a strong case for the opposite view.

CLARK KERR

Wage Relationships—
The Comparative Impact of Market
and Power Forces*

Although its title implies treatment of the whole issue of the relative effect of market and power forces, this paper quickly narrows to a summary appraisal of the degree of union influence on wages. The term "wages" is too unwieldy for careful analysis, so that the impact of unionism is related to five separate wage structures—interpersonal, interfirm, interarea, interoccupational, and interindustry.

Within this framework Kerr addresses himself to the broader problem of union influence on wages in general rather than the narrower one of the effect of unionism in raising wages. His summary conclusions based on the existing evidence on variations within wage structures are that unions try to equalize wages among covered workers who make equal contributions and that the effect of this policy is dependent on the effort expended and opposition met. Kerr finds that wage differentials within all structures have narrowed historically and that unions have had varying degrees of influence on the individual structures. Kerr maintains that they have been most successful in equalizing wages at the interpersonal and interfirm level, have had indifferent success in the interarea field, and have had little or no influence in the narrowing trend of occupational and industrial wage structures.

O NE modern version of Adam Smith's famous observation (Book I, Chapter 8) might read: "Workmen are always in constant and uniform combination to raise the wages of labour above their

* Reprinted by permission from John T. Dunlop, ed., *The Theory of Wage Determination,* by permission of the Macmillan Company Ltd. and Saint Martin's Press.

actual rate." Now this version would not be so true as Smith's about "masters" (as Smith himself noted), for their combination is less the "natural state of things." Workers, being more numerous and diverse, have less of a community of interest than masters and a greater need for formal bonds. These formal bonds, over the past century, have been supplied by labour unions in many trades and industries in those industrialized nations which are organized into pluralistic systems, and a major purpose of most of these unions has been to modify "market forces" by group decisions and organized power in setting wages.

A classic question in economics has been the extent to which this organized power has exerted its will over market forces. Some economists in recent times have judged the impact to be substantial and even potentially disastrous; others that it has been minimal or even virtually non-existent. This chapter concludes, on our current state of knowledge, that no categorical answer can be given because unions have had varying degrees of impact on the five different types of differentials into which a nation's wage structure can be divided: (1) interpersonal, (2) interfirm, (3) interarea, (4) interoccupational, and (5) interindustry. The impact on the first two, it will be found, has been considerably greater than on the last two. We must then turn to an explanation of why the impact should vary so substantially; why there should be such a shift in the incidence of trade union power from one set of differentials to the other. The answer given is that a sharp downward plunge in motivation and an equally sharp upward surge of the power requisite to effect alterations in differentials occur as we move from the first three (and particularly the first two) to the last two.

The customary dichotomy of "market" and "power" forces lacks full precision. "Power forces" often work through the market as well as on price directly; and "market forces" themselves contain elements of power to the extent that persons or groups can and do directly influence the demand or supply side of the market. It might be more useful to speak of "individual responses" on the one hand and "institutional behaviour" on the other.[1]

---

[1] Lester divides the forces at work into "competitive," "impeditive," and "anticompetitive." The first category includes competitive drives among companies but also among unions. The second includes the standard "frictions" of lack of knowledge, personal attachments, and so forth. The third includes a miscellany of practices such as pattern following by an employer and restriction of entrance to the trade by the union. R. A. Lester, "A Range Theory of Wage Differentials," *Industrial and Labor Relations Review* (July 1952).

"Individual responses" are the expressed preferences of individual workers and unorganized employers in response to the environmental context in which they find themselves. While in totality their actions affect the result, their individual actions taken separately do not succeed in manipulating their environment. "Institutional behaviour" is comprised of the policies and practices of groups of individuals in the dominant corporation, the employers' association, the trade union, or government.

When a market responds largely to the first type of action, it might be designated as a "natural" market, however imperfect it may be aside from collusive action itself; and when to the latter, an "institutional" market. Most actual markets will, of course, have characteristics of both of these types; and then some evaluation is in order of the comparative influence of these two types of forces. Our question is then, to rephrase it, to what extent have wage differentials been affected by the entry of "institutional behaviour," in addition to "individual responses," into the supply side of the labour market; and how may the varying extents be explained.

I. WAGE DIFFERENTIALS

Interpersonal Differentials

Institutional policy quite universally regularizes, when it does not eliminate, differentials among persons doing like work in the same plant — with one sometimes quite major exception. The differentials may be regularized by a piece-rate system, or by seniority increments, or by a formal method of merit recognition, if a flat rate for the work is not introduced. The union contract, the company job evaluation system, and government wage regulations all have the effect of banishing the purely personalized rate. Such personalized rates, reflecting the merit of the worker or the prejudices of the individual foreman or employer, are quite normal in the "natural market."

"Job selling" by foremen, wage discrimination by supervisors, and the secrecy of individual arrangements have given way to formalized rates for the job. The movement toward centralization of hiring by employers and the experience in several countries with governmental wage controls have aided this change, as well as trade union pressure. While statistical proof of union influence is largely lacking, at least one study in the United States indicates a close association between unionization and formal wage structures. "Individual rates" are most common in those areas where unionism is not influential. Formalized wage structures were shown, also, to be closely associated with increasing size of the enterprise.

The one important exception is differentials between men and women doing the same work. These have been largely eradicated in the United States, particularly during the 1940's, but they are still customary in some other countries, such as Germany.[2] The degree of elimination may well relate more to the general social status of women in the community than to union influence.

Interfirm Differentials

In the absence of unionism, the labour market normally displays a wide dispersion of wage rates for the same type of work among firms operating in the same product and labour markets. Lester, on the basis of data for some sixty-odd cities in the United States, generalized that the high wage plant normally paid 50 per cent more in rates, occupation by occupation, than the low wage plant. The findings of Reynolds in his New Haven survey are consistent with this, although they relate to more than a single industry at a time. The Lester data were taken from a period of turbulent wage movements during the second World War. But numerous wage surveys covering less unusual times demonstrate a normal dispersion, odd stragglers aside, of at least 25 per cent from top to bottom.

While union policy does not always aim at full uniformity, unionization is closely associated with increased uniformity. Two recent studies in the United States have noted this. One found a considerably lower dispersion of rates in the more highly unionized of two metropolitan areas. The other concluded that within a single metropolitan area, namely Los Angeles, unions reduced and even abolished interfirm differentials in the industries they organized.

This phenomenon is not limited to the United States. It occurs wherever unions are able to organize all the firms producing the same product in the same labour market area. In fact, it may be more manifest in other nations where the "master agreement" has met less employer resistance than in the United States. In some countries, as Germany, the "master agreement" is even extended by law to cover all

---

[2] They have, however, been regularized there in the sense of being made subject to contractual arrangements. (See C. Kerr, "Collective Bargaining in Post-War Germany," *Industrial and Labor Relations Review*, April 1952.) In Germany and some other countries there are also established differentials for youths below the regular rates.

employers. The achievement of this uniformity is an essential part of the union programme of "taking wages out of competition." It flows also from activities of employers' associations and the application of government minimum wage regulations.

Interarea Differentials

What are usually called "geographical differentials" are, in part, inter-industry differentials in the sense that the industry mix varies from one area to another and for this reason alone the general average of wages would be expected to vary; and, in part, real geographical differentials in the sense that different rates are paid for the same type of work. The term "interarea differentials" is used here in the second sense of relative rates of pay for the same kind of work in the same industry but in different geographical areas. Here union policy has generally favoured the reduction or elimination of differentials, particularly where there is an interarea product market.

In the United States, interarea differentials have been narrowing gradually both over-all and industry by industry. This is probably largely due, as Reynolds notes, to the increased dispersion of manufacturing industry around the nation and the reduced importance in some areas of a large localized supply of agricultural workers. In some industries with nation-wide markets, such as steel, automobiles, and meat packing, union agreements have brought a reduction or elimination of geographical differentials. In other industries with local product markets, like building trades and service trades, no similar result has been attempted or achieved.[3]

Oxnam describes a similar narrowing of differentials among the several states in Australia, but does not relate this to union policy. In Germany, where highly formalized wage structures are subject to well-developed collective arrangements, interarea differentials (including urban-rural differentials) have either been eliminated or substantially narrowed and precisely prescribed.

Evidence about the impact of unionism on interarea differentials is less conclusive than for interpersonal and interfirm differentials. Union pressure generally is directed towards the narrowing and regularization of such differentials, but the over-all effect certainly has been substantially less than in the case of the first two types of differentials.

---

[3] On a less spectacular level, unions have often raised wage rates for the same type of work in the same industry in labour market areas adjacent to the metropolitan districts where they first establish their organizational strength.

Interoccupational Differentials

Occupational wage differentials have undergone a most significant narrowing in recent decades in the United States, Western Europe, Australia, and New Zealand, with one very important exception.[4] In the United States the margin for skilled workers has dropped over the past half-century from over two to under one and one-half times that of unskilled workers. Since 1880, in the United Kingdom, the differential has also been cut in half, although it was not so great to begin with. An almost equal reduction has occurred in Australia over the period since 1914. In more recent periods, reductions have occurred in Austria, France, Germany, Italy, Netherlands, Norway, and Switzerland, and also New Zealand. The great exception, and a most interesting one, is Denmark (another possible one — although the evidence is less complete — is Belgium). In Denmark the differential did not narrow over the period 1938–1948, nor from 1920 to 1949, although it did decrease substantially from 1914 to 1920.

This narrowing of occupational differentials has been an important massive and highly controversial social phenomenon. Turner views trade unions as a substantial causative force, as unions follow the policy of flat increases, as they seek to recruit to their ranks the unskilled, as they endeavour to avoid undue incentives to employers to break down skills and use machines, and as they pursue egalitarian policies to minimize internal strife. Knowles and Robertson, however, see unions as having a relatively minor and largely unpurposeful effect as they support, for other reasons, flat increases and the simplification of wage structures. Reynolds and Samuels consider the impact of unionism a temporary one as organization first spreads from the ranks of the skilled to the unskilled. Fisher and Clark find the explanation for reduced differentials lying almost entirely outside unionism in the spread of public education and its effect on the relative supply of skilled and unskilled workers. Among other explanatory factors have been listed the impact of full employment in raising the demand for the unskilled, of mass technology which reduces the level of skill, of egalitarian tendencies generally which are expressed in many ways, including state minimum wage regulations.

---

[4] What has happened to "compensation" differentials (wages and "fringe benefits" taken together) is a different and more complex question; and an increasingly important one with the growth of "fringe benefits." The "compensation structure" is a more meaningful, if less tractable, concept than the "wage structure." On the currently available evidence it is almost foolhardy to estimate whether occupational "compensation" differentials are or are not behaving similarly to occupational wage differentials.

As to the weight to be given these several factors, there is little incontrovertible evidence. My own view, which will be set forth below, is that the impact of unionism is seldom the major factor involved; and that, in the long run, its influence is generally in the direction of maintaining, not reducing, occupational differentials.

Interindustry Differentials

Clay wrote that there had once been a "system" of wages in Great Britain. It might almost be said that there is a "system" of wages which operates in a recognizable form in a number of the industrialized nations — not an entirely uniform and constant system, it is true, but one according to which the several series of interrelationships are roughly similar. It is the variations, not the likenesses, which call for explanation. Lebergott found interindustry rankings, with a few major exceptions, to be much the same in six countries (United States, Canada, United Kingdom, Sweden, Switzerland, Russia); and the Economic Commission for Europe study shows somewhat the same pattern.

A second general observation about interindustry differentials is that they are narrowing (percentagewise) over time. Oxnam has demonstrated this for Australia, Woytinsky for the United States, and the Economic Commission for Europe study for Western European countries.

Has unionism had an appreciable effect on these differentials?[5] Douglas thought it had not as between unionized and unorganized industries. Ross at first challenged the observation of Douglas, but later agreed that, except in the case of new organizations (a point made also by Douglas), unionism has had little appreciable effect in the United States. Essentially similar results to those of Douglas have been obtained by Garbarino, Rees (for the steel industry only), and Dunlop, all also having analysed American experience. Levinson essentially agrees, except that unions may hold up the level of wages in an organized industry in a depression when wages in unorganized industries are not faring as well. Sobotka, further, reached the judgment, after a study of the building trades, that craft unions may be a source of wage advantage to their members. The three likely excep-

---

[5] Actually there are two questions: (1) Has unionism been a source of comparative advantage to workers in unionized as contrasted with unorganized industries?; and (2) Has unionism changed the pattern of relationships among organized industries? The literature is almost solely concerned with the first of these two questions, partly because it has been the more debated point and partly because statistical evidence is more easily procured.

tions to the general rule that unionism has not been a source of wage
advantage to workers in organized industries, then, are (1) new and
thus aggressive unions (which may also be offsetting the prior monopsony power of employers); (2) unions in periods of substantial unemployment; and (3) craft unions with their restrictions on entrance
to the trade.[6]

It is evident from this review of the literature and the available
data (both of which relate more to the United States than to any
other country) that the impact of unionism on wage differentials has
not been uniform:

(1) Personal differentials have largely been eliminated or brought
under formal control in unionized sectors.

(2) Firm differentials within the same product and labour markets
have generally either been much reduced or wiped out.

(3) Area differentials have been occasionally eradicated and
frequently diminished, particularly where there is interarea product
competition.

(4) Occupational differentials have been much reduced, but there
is little evidence that this is a result of union policies.

(5) Industrial differentials have also been reduced, but have
apparently not been greatly affected to date by unionism.

For the first two types of differentials the impact of unionism has
been substantial; for the third (at least in the limited situation of
interarea product competition), significant; and for the last two,
minor.

The intrusion of unionism into labour markets does not present
a clear-cut case of "market forces" versus "power". For the power
of the union is sometimes ranged alongside the market forces and
they work in the same direction. Also, the opposition to union
power may not be market forces, or market forces alone, but the
power of the employers or the government. We turn now to a
general explanation of why union power has been more effective in
transforming some aspects of the wage structure than others.

[6] This may be a finding largely related to American experience; and the
factor in American experience which may most count for the special results
of craft unions is their comparatively heavy emphasis on the closed shop and
the partially closed union. In Denmark also, where the craft unions have close
historical connections with the craft guilds of earlier times and their tight
apprenticeship systems, they apparently have also been a source of differential
advantage.

II. THE SELECTIVE IMPACT OF UNION POWER

Is there any general explanation of why union power has achieved so much rearrangement of some wage differentials and so little of others? The explanation offered here is that the impact of unionism on wage differentials has varied (1) directly with the strength of the motivation of workers and their organizations to exercise control, and (2) inversely with the amount of power requisite to effect such changes.[7] It would, of course, be surprising if this were not true. What, then, can we say about intensity of motivation and the magnitude of power requirements in each of the five types of differentials which constitute wage structures?

As we shall see, where motivation is most intense, power requirements tend to be least in magnitude. Were it otherwise, trade unionism would have to endure much greater frustrations; for what it could best achieve it would least want, and what it most wanted it could least achieve.

The Intensity of Motivation

The idea of the "just wage" has never died, although the meaning of justice in this regard is perhaps less clear than it once was and there are many more wage rates to be adjusted one to the other. The "just wage," it is often remarked, is largely an ethical rather than an "economic" concept. But one purpose of organization, as in the Middle Ages, is to make it both. Now this is not to suggest that this is the only purpose of organization in the labour market, nor that the customary appeals to justice are always sincere, but only that the achievement of justice, however defined, is a real and major goal. This is particularly true in the early days of unionism. The drive to end discrimination, to get "equal pay for equal work," to obtain the "standard rate," is behind the original organization of many, if not most unions.

This drive for the "standard rate" is particularly insistent at the level of interpersonal relationships in the same work place. Workers are physically close to each other and comparisons are easy to make. It is less forceful but still quite intense as it relates to interfirm differentials in the same labour and product markets. Here the incentive comes not from one worker eyeing another at the next

[7] It should be noted that power and motivation are not entirely independent factors. The degree of power required may affect motivation; and the intensity of motivation may affect the amount of power available.

bench, but from workers in low-wage plants thinking they are worth as much as those in high-wage plants and the workers in high-wage plants feeling uneasy about unfair competition possibly threatening their jobs. Considerations of equity for the one group and security for the other move hand in hand. The motivation is more a result of thought processes and less one of glandular response than in the case of interpersonal differentials for the same jobs in the same plant.

When we move out of the same labour market area, the strength of the inducements to uniformity subsides. Knowledge of the total situation is less personal and less complete, comparisons are made on a less individual basis, similarities are less striking — the cost of living may be different, market conditions diverse, and so forth. Particularly when product market competition is less intense or even non-existent, the interest in uniformity is much reduced, although the equity of interarea relationships may still be a factor; but the coercion of wage competition is absent.

When we turn to occupational differentials the character of the situation changes quickly. Dissimilarity is now the essence of the problem. Degrees of skill, of responsibility, of unpleasantness must be estimated and weighed, and this takes intimate knowledge and careful judgment. Equal pay for equal work gives way to equivalent pay for equivalent work; and there is little agreement on what is equivalent.[8] While workers may generally agree that there should be the same pay for the same type of work in the same plant, labour market area, or industry, motives become mixed within the work force in regard to appropriate occupational differentials. The unskilled wish equality or some close approximation; the skilled want to be differentiated on the grounds of their skill.

Thus almost no unions in the United States have a general policy on skill differentials, as Bell notes, although nearly all have definite policies, however imperfectly enforced, on interpersonal, interfirm, and interarea differentials. It is often said that craft unions favour the skilled workers and industrial unions the unskilled. But this is certainly not universally true. Industrial unions must be sensitive to potential revolts of their skilled members, and skilled workers quite normally are influential in an industrial union beyond their relative numbers. The differential between skilled and unskilled

[8] As skills become more diversified with the progressive division of labour, particularly at the semi-skilled level, comparisons become increasingly difficult to make. See R. L. Raimon, "The Indeterminativeness of Wages of Semi-skilled Workers," *Industrial and Labor Relations Review* (January 1953).

workers in the construction industry (organized on a craft basis) in the United States has narrowed over recent decades much more than in the steel and somewhat more than in the automobile industries (organized on an industrial basis). In the steel industry a formal contractual job evaluation plan sets differentials, and in the automobile industry special adjustments for skilled workers have been made to offset the effect of flat cents-per-hour increases. Industrial unions too, with very few exceptions, are hierarchical organizations.

In Denmark the skilled workers, after a time, resisted further reductions in their differentials, although they had once supported a "solidaristic" wage policy. In Norway and Sweden the unions have maintained a policy of improving "the relative position of traditionally low-paid groups of workers"; but the statistical evidence does not indicate that this policy has had the effect of narrowing differentials more rapidly than was occurring in other comparable nations. In the Netherlands the Foundation of Labour (a joint employer-union organization) has endeavoured to maintain (not reduce) occupational differentials in the post-war period at their approximate pre-war relationship, but apparently without substantial success, for the wages of the unskilled have in fact risen much faster than those of the skilled.

Unions may, however, unwittingly have had two effects on occupational differentials. First, the organization of the skilled may originally have spread differentials a bit and the subsequent organization of the unskilled narrowed them again; and, second, across-the-board and pattern increases, particularly as applied by industrial unions, may have reduced them somewhat. But neither of these results generally has grown out of deliberate policy on occupational differentials *per se*.

Interindustry differentials confront unions with much the same problems of unclear motivation as do occupational differentials. New elements of dissimilarity enter in — different families of occupations, working conditions, product market arrangements, among many others. Here, also, the workers in the highly paid industries wish normally to maintain their relative superiority, however much those in the low-paid industries might wish to narrow the gap.

Thus, in summary, the unions speak with a distinct although decreasingly loud voice on interpersonal, interfirm, and interarea differentials; but in halting tones, if at all, on interoccupational and interindustry differentials. A great drop in strong and unambiguous motivation takes place as they move from "equal work" to "unequal work" situations. The "equal work" orbits are generally the most coercive.[9]

The Variation in Power Requirements

Group motivation to be effective must be expressed through the exercise of power, and this power may need to be exercised not only against "market forces" but also against the opposing power of organized employers or the state, and even against discordant factions internal to the union institution. Thus the power required to effect changes is not just the opposite of the strength of market forces.

At the level of interpersonal differentials the individual employer usually stands alone — and confused. On the one hand, he may like his prerogatives, including the right to reward those who gain his favour or whose work merits it; but, on the other, a formal wage schedule reduces grumbling, is easier to administer (particularly for the large firm) than a person-by-person rate system, and has some obvious ethical appeal to it. Moreover the employer, who is likely to pay more attention to personal differences in productivity than the union, can make some relatively easy adjustments to adapt to the "standard rate" by eliminating the poorer workers or by forcing them to raise their output.

Interfirm differentials are more difficult for a union to assault. Now it must organize similar firms in the entire labour market area. But the union is not without aid and comfort from the enemy. High wage firms may accept or even welcome union action to raise the wages of their low-wage competitors; and uniformity of wage levels is often a necessary prerequisite to uniformity of price in the product market — with or without union support. Moreover, uniformity of wage levels can be as essential to the internal harmony of an employers' association as it is to a union; and tactics in bargaining with an aggressive union dictate removal of the "whipsaw" approach of first raising the low-wage firms in the name of equality and then the high-wage firms in the name of preserving historical positions.

Once uniformity is achieved there is normally little to destroy it, at least at the "official" level. Effective rates, however, under conditions which favour the "wage slide" (to be noted below) may

[9] This is not to suggest that political forces, like rival unionism, may not be of pre-eminent importance in individual situations. For an interesting discussion of such "orbits of coercive comparison" see A. M. Ross, "The Dynamics of Wage Determination Under Collective Bargaining," *American Economic Review* (September 1947).

depart, even substantially, from the "official" level. The low-wage firms have either been eliminated or have become efficient enough to survive at the standard rate; and unions do not normally press for wage rates which would force unionized employers to cease operations or break with the union. A standard rate, too, and perhaps one at much the same level, might well be the result of market forces if the labour market were more perfect than it usually is. Unionization, instead of "distorting" the interfirm wage structure, may act instead as a substitute for greater labour mobility.

The reduction or removal of interarea differentials demands an additional accumulation of power by the union. To be effective the union now must organize beyond a single labour market area, even on a national basis. In a large country, such as the United States, this may be quite difficult, and peculiarly so if there are regions which are especially hard to organize, like the southern states; and, in the absence of complete organization, plants may be able to run away from one area to another. Also the union must either negotiate contracts on an interarea basis, or be able to establish effective policy for its local branches negotiating area by area. Moreover, employers, if product market competition is confined to local labour markets, will normally uniformly oppose, even strenuously, the standardization of wages among different product markets. Also, wage differentials tend to be more widely dispersed over a series of labour markets than in a single market, and thus less tractable to standardization. But the state may enter here and range its power alongside that of the unions through minimum wage laws or laws on the extension of contracts; and wherever labour mobility is increasing and product markets are widening, "market forces" are also conducing toward uniformity.

As far as occupational differentials are concerned, something can be done about them quite readily at the plant or industry level, and in totality this can have some effect. This can be done consciously or almost inadvertently, as Knowles and Robertson comment, through policies of the flat increase and simplification of the wage structure which are intended to serve other purposes. But occupational differentials, given the occupational diversity among industries, are, in part, also interindustry differentials. Consequently, in order to control occupational differentials generally, as interpersonal and interplant and sometimes interarea differentials are controlled, would require a national union federation with considerable influence over its constituent elements. What is requisite is a single policy covering the building trades, the textile industry, and many others, all at the same time. Perhaps only in Norway and Sweden do the union federations have this much power, if they wish to use it.

A great social force is at work on occupational differentials. This force is the changing nature of supply and demand in the labour market as industrialization progresses. The absolute demand for skilled workers is certainly larger in an advanced industrial state than in one entering industrialization; but the need for skilled workers is much more critical in a nation undergoing industrialization, and particularly in one where the process is rapid.[10] Percentagewise, the additional need for skilled men is much reduced as industrial societies mature. In Russia, for example, in 1928, skill differentials about matched those in the United States a quarter of a century earlier, and then widened as the first five-year plan speeded up the process of industrialization.[11] Concurrently with the smaller percentage increase in demand for skilled workers, as industrialization becomes well established, the supply of skilled workers greatly increases through the effects of public education, and perhaps also a concomitant reduction of class or social discrimination, while the supply of unskilled workers dries up as agriculture becomes a smaller segment of the economy, as income and the trade and service industries draws also on the ranks of the unskilled.

We may, in fact, be witnessing currently a great social phenomenon of occupational differentials being turned partly on their heads. Already they have been greatly narrowed and in some cases reversed, as, for example, when common labourers come to receive more than skilled office workers.[12] If this is the social process at work, then we should not be surprised that the narrowing of differentials

[10] The general theorem advanced here is: The lesser the degree and the greater the rate of industrialization, the wider will be the occupational differentials and the greater the premium for skill; and the greater the degree and the lesser the rate of industrialization, the narrower will be the occupational differentials and the greater the premium for distasteful work.

[11] A. Bergson, *The Structure of Soviet Wages* (1946). Bendix also notes a widening of skill differentials in the Russian zone of Germany with the Russian emphasis on industrial expansion there after the second World War. See R. Bendix, *Managerial Ideologies in the Russian Orbit of Germany,* unpublished MS. (1953). Skill differentials are rather greater in the United States than one would normally expect for a country at its stage of development. Large-scale immigration undoubtedly held down the level for unskilled workers for a substantial time and the differentials are particularly wide in the South which is industrially under-developed.

[12] For a discussion of the narrowing of the white-collar manual worker differential over the past century in the United States see K. M. McCaffree, "The Earnings Differential between White Collar and Manual Occupations," *Review of Economics and Statistics* (February 1953). This differential has narrowed

has not caused a shortage of skilled workers, for their comparative plenitude has, in fact, caused the narrowing.[13] Adam Smith's first wage-determining factor (Book I, Chapter 10), "the agreeableness or disagreeableness of the employments themselves," may come to be a most influential one once the "difficulty and expense of learning them" have been much more equalized; and, it should be noted, unskilled work is quite frequently more disagreeable than skilled.

Unions have probably not had much effect on the historical narrowing of occupational differentials. These differentials began narrowing in some countries before unions were effective and have narrowed since that time in non-union sectors as well as organized sectors. The movement has not been at a uniform rate but has gone in spurts, particularly during the first and second World Wars. Once having narrowed under the pressure of full or overly-full employment, the differentials have not dropped back to their prior relationships in periods of less than full employment.[14] The long-run trend has worked itself out partly gradually and partly in these forward jumps.

In the future, however, unionism may well be an impediment to further narrowing, as it protects the position of skilled workers in particular and as it stands generally for a continuation of established and formalized differentials perpetuated through contractual arrangements and the development of conventional patterns. Already this has happened in Denmark, as noted above, where craft unions are particularly strong,[15] and for a substantial period of time (1920–1950)

more rapidly in the United States than in some other countries, like Germany, where a "closed education" system based on class lines has protected white-collar employees just as the "closed shop" has craft workers in the United States.

[13] See A. Flanders, "Wage Policy and Full Employment in Britain," *Bulletin of the Oxford University Institute of Statistics* (July and August 1950). See also comment in Lester, "A Range Theory of Wage Differentials." It is sometimes argued that skilled workers must be in relatively shorter supply than unskilled workers because the unskilled in a depression make up a disproportionate number of the unemployed. But this can be explained by a general pushing down of workers and those on the bottom, the unskilled, go out.

[14] This long-term trend explains why P. W. Bell ("Cyclical Variation and Trend in Occupational Wage Differentials in American Industry Since 1914," *Review of Economics and Statistics*, November, 1951) did not observe a widening of occupational differentials in depression periods. The standard statement is that the differentials narrow in prosperity and widen in depression. Because of the effect of this long-run trend, the former is true, but not the latter.

[15] Walter Galeson, *The Danish System of Labor Relations* (1952), also notes that "nationwide bargaining on the Danish model creates a propensity

in Australia, where government wage setting is of pre-eminent importance; and it has been attempted in the Netherlands.

Interindustry differentials may well follow the same course as occupational differentials. They also are narrowing and a long-run reversal is taking place in interindustry relationships in favour of those industries, like mining, where the work has heavy disutility factors connected with it. Such a parallel development is to be expected because interindustry differentials are, in significant part, skill differentials.[16] This is particularly true at the extremes. The high-ranking industries historically have been industries with many skilled workers; the low-ranking industries have been industries with many semi-skilled and unskilled workers (and usually also a high proportion of women). The contribution of the skill mix to the wage

toward rigidity in wage structure" (p. 186). It is my own view, albeit somewhat heretical, that, in the long run, industrial unions may often grant more protection to skill than craft unions, despite the early cry of industrial unions that they are the special benefactors of the unskilled. This is, first, because industrial unions gather within the same decision-making unit both unskilled and skilled rates and thus can subject them simultaneously to control; while craft unions usually leave the unskilled on the outside in other decision-making units less subject to control. Industrial unions thus can hold the rates for the skilled and the unskilled apart if they wish and usually they will, since the skilled workers are the long-service workers and the most influential members. Craft unions cannot really hold the rates apart because only one set of rates — those for the skilled — fall within their control. The width of the gap is the distance between two levels, only one of which the craft unions can control. Second, under the craft system, both the unskilled and skilled rates are "in the market" and the unskilled rate by itself must be high enough to permit adequate recruiting; while, under the industrial system, the combined rate structure does the recruiting. That is to say, unskilled workers are attracted not only by the unskilled rates but also by the skilled rates to which they may expect to advance through time and the operation of a seniority plan. Just as the unskilled rate can be somewhat lower because of the prospect of higher rates ahead, so also the skilled rates are "out of competition" in the sense that recruiting is usually from within and not from the open market and it can be "artificially" high without being very obvious.

[16] See S. Lebergott, "Wage Structures," *Review of Economic Statistics* (November, 1947), on the association between skilled and unskilled rates, industry by industry; also Slichter, "Notes on the Structure of Wages," *Review of Economics and Statistics* (January 1950), also Deneffe, "The Wage Structure of the Federal Republic," *Wirtschaft und Statistik* (July 1953) — for example, the high rates of cleaning-women in the coal mines. Similarly a big and high wage industry (like automobiles in Detroit or shipbuilding in Hamburg) may pull up low-wage industries in its area, and vice versa.

levels of the several industries is also indicated by the similarity in interindustry wage differentials among countries where other potentially influential factors, like the organization of workers or the structures of product markets, are quite diverse. Additionally, the narrowing and reversal of rank order of interindustry differentials can best be explained by the narrowing and reversal of rank order of occupational differentials.

The skill mix, while it is probably the basic underlying force in determining interindustry differentials, is not the only important factor. Ability to pay, influenced by many factors, including the concentration of production, is of very substantial importance.[17] So also is the secular expansion or contraction of employment for particular industries at particular times, the geographical location of different industries and their cyclical price sensitivity, among other factors. Factors other than occupational differentials are probably particularly important for the series of industries between the extremes of those with a high skill mix and those with a low. Thus, just as occupational differentials affect interindustry differentials, so also changes in interindustry differentials (for reasons other than changes in occupational differentials) will, in turn, affect occupational differentials.

If the narrowing (and scrambling) of occupational differentials is to continue to cause a narrowing (and scrambling) of interindustry differentials,[18] what effect is unionism likely to have on this process? Probably the major effect is in the direction of preserving differentials, once established, because of the penchant for pattern following. Organizational pride and leadership survival are often intimately linked to the preservation of established wage relationships. But the pattern is seldom followed exactly; the economic situations of industries do change over time; and so do interindustry wage differentials, whether through changes in negotiated wage levels or through the process of individual employers bidding for labour, particularly during high peaks or low troughs of the business cycle, despite union

[17] See, for example, J. W. Garbarino, "A Theory of Interindustry Wage Structure Variation," *Quarterly Journal of Economics* (May, 1950), and Slichter, "Notes on the Structure of Wages." It appears likely that control of entrance into the labour market and reduction of competition in the product market raise wage rates more effectively above the "natural" level than does direct bargaining pressure; restriction and collusion open more doors for gain than the strike.

[18] The reduction of regional variations has also served to narrow interindustry differentials in the United States.

inclinations to formalize them.[19] What other effects may unions have on interindustry differentials? They cannot assure an advantage to organized industries over unorganized, because, among other reasons, non-union employers can follow right along. Nor can they control differentials among organized industries except through very substantial centralized power over their member elements, and then only if they can also impose their will on the employers.

The amount of power requisite to control or even to influence differentials increases precipitately as we pass from the simple case of interpersonal differentials on through to the complex one of interindustry differentials. The purpose of the application of power changes also from highly consciously attempted elimination of interpersonal, interfirm, and interarea differentials to less consciously attempted stabilization of interoccupational and interindustry differentials, and, thus, from egalitarian reform to caste-conscious rigidity. The slogans associated with the former sometimes obscure the contribution to the latter. Appearance and reality go their separate ways.

As a union movement adds to its power it would be expected to penetrate effectively first into the control of interpersonal differentials (where the motivation is also the strongest) and last into interindustry differentials (where the motivation is also much reduced). The degree of effective penetration into control of wage differentials is, also, one measure of the true power of unions.

We remarked earlier that what the unions and their members most wanted they could best secure. Also, where the unions are consequential, they are also largely beneficial (in that they help achieve results which would flow from full employment and more perfect labour and product markets); and where they are less beneficial (impeding the rearrangement of differentials encouraged by the equalization of opportunity which tends to accompany industrialization), they are also less consequential.

What effect, then, does unionism have on the over-all distribution of wage and salary earnings among persons? The pattern of earnings distribution must change greatly as industrialization progresses, although statistics are largely lacking to demonstrate this. In Stage One there must be (assuming a substantial number of agricultural labourers) a heavy concentration of persons at the low end of the distribution. In Stage Two a second "hump" appears

[19] In Denmark, however, the unions have had remarkable success in maintaining almost unchanged for a substantial period of time intercraft (which in Denmark are also in large part interindustry) wage differentials. See Galenson, *The Danish System*, p. 181.

at the high end of the scale as skilled "aristocrats of labour" are recruited. In Stage Three a third "hump" appears in the middle representing the semi-skilled and this "hump" grows and grows. In Stage Four only one "hump" is left — in the centre — as the unskilled have their rates raised and the skilled their rates relatively reduced; and inside this "hump" some skilled jobs shift to the left of the distribution (like white-collar occupations) and some less skilled jobs (like coal mining) shift to the right. The effects of unions on this historical process are probably as follows: (1) to pull up the very low rates a bit (by eliminating the low-paying firms and areas or forcing them to pay more); and (2) to hold up the high rates a bit against the pressures for narrowing; and (3), within the "hump," to stand as an element of rigidity against the transposition of rates from one side to the other. But, in totality, they lack the influence to effect, through collective bargaining, a major redistribution of income among persons.

Böhm-Bawerk, forty years ago, as many had before and even more have since, discussed this same problem. He set in opposition to each other "power" and "natural economic laws" and posed the issue: "The great problem, not adequately settled so far, is to determine the exact extent and nature of the influence of both factors, to show how much one factor may accomplish apart from, and perhaps in opposition to, the other." His main illustration was from the labour market and his conclusion was that, with a few exceptions,[20] "there is, in my opinion, not a single instance where the influence of control could be lasting as against the gently and slowly, but incessantly and therefore successfully, working influence of a 'purely economic order.'"

The problem is still not adequately settled and may never be, for we are working with a very tangled web of forces. The answer offered here is that neither market forces (or what we have called "individual responses") have basically governed in fact nor is power, or perhaps more accurately "institutional behavior," the compelling force which has determined wage differentials.

The problem is too complex for a single reply. Union policies have often brought major, and presumably permanent changes in two of the differentials we have examined — personal and firm; and have had some, and presumably also permanent effects on area differentials. They have not evidently, however, been a dominant factor

[20] The main exception was where union power offset the pre-existing monopsony power of employers.

affecting the other two — occupational and industrial. The general explanation given here is that the degree of penetration of trade union influence into the establishment and maintenance of wage differentials is related directly to the intensity and clarity of the motivations of the workers and their organizations, and inversely to the amount of power requisite to the task.

COMMENT

In the previous selection, Kerr is reluctant to use the terms "market forces" and "power forces" because of the overlapping influence they sometimes exert. Kerr's terms, "individual responses" and "institutional behavior" have the quality of seeming to have separate and independent meanings. Unfortunately, the distinct difference in meaning of the two expressions cannot be applied in the determination of the extent to which union efforts influence wage levels and wage structure variations. To the degree that union wage pressure is sometimes in the direction of market forces, it would be difficult to establish whether a particular wage movement resulted more from individual responses or institutional behavior (union activity). A rise in wages, for example, may result from union pressure or rising labor demand during prosperous periods. In another case, a differential wage rise in favor of unionized firms might occur when demand shifts to these firms.

Kerr is aware of the confusion in assigning causes resulting from the dynamic implications of wage setting. For example, the presence of relatively higher wages among unionized firms in an industry might truly reflect greater bargaining pressure applied by these firms than the market wage pressures among the unorganized firms; however, higher wage firms might be more susceptible to organization than lower wage firms so that the organization of the high wage firms might have reflected favorable market conditions for organization. Thus, the increasing wage differential between the industry's unionized and unorganized sector might reflect the greater strength of "institutional behavior" or power forces, over "individual responses" or market forces, but the very existence of the power forces themselves might have developed out of antecedent market conditions.

According to Kerr's presentation, union wage activity is centered on the equalization, or standardization, of wages within structures. This policy is based on worker interest in ending differential rates by comparable effort. This same standardizing tendency of union wage policy has been noted by Arthur Ross in his *Trade Union Wage Policy,* but Ross emphasizes that this tendency is the result of membership interest in attaining equality in wages within labor markets. To Ross a labor market, as such, is a meaningless factor in the determination of union wage policy. He speaks of "orbits of coercive comparison," the factors that bind workers in common wage goals. To the extent that workers feel their wages should be equal to those of other workers, either because they are in the same firm, industry, or same locality, as examples, unions are obligated to try to achieve equality in order to hold the support of their membership.

This position is stressed below in a summary statement of Ross' chapter (article), "The Dynamics of Wage Determination Under Collective Bargaining," in his *Trade Union Wage Policy* (University of California Press, 1950, pp. 72–74). This brief selection is included not only because of its presentation from a leading spokesman of the power forces school of the view of unions as a wage-standardizing agent, but also because of its eloquent rhetoric in defense of this view.

Despite the popularity of analogies from physics, economic behavior remains perversely intractable to mechanical analysis. Within the several branches of economic theory this is nowhere better illustrated than in the theory of wages and collective bargaining. The apparatus of equilibrium analysis has been adopted in its entirety. Wages are the "price of labor," established in the "labor market." Collective bargaining is "bilateral monopoly"; the union is a monopolistic seller of labor. Wages emerge from the interaction of supply and demand in the labor market. In order to complete the analogy, it is held that competition among buyers and sellers of labor integrates and unifies the wage structure, whereas imperfect competition among buyers and sellers inhibits the tendency toward equalization of wage rates.

Formally the parallel appears reasonably good. Much could be overlooked if the analysis worked well, and if, as sometimes happens, more or less correct conclusions were reached from false premises. But if current wage doctrine is conceptually unsound, practically it is impossible. The results are poor and the lacunae manifold. Where one price should prevail in the labor market, there are many. Labor market theorists are so burdened with the task of identifying rigidities and imperfections that little time has been left to make a constructive theoretical reformulation. On balance, the labor market concept is a net liability in wage analysis; there is a fatal disjunction between the spatially limited character of supply and demand and the spatially unlimited characteristics of wage determination under collective bargaining.

We are not enlightened on the reasons why unions demand what they do, why employers grant what they do, and why arbitrators award what they do. We are told that the wage structure is a living, breathing organism, but its way of life remains a mystery. Viewed in the large, what is euphemistically called our "national wage structure" is a maze of distinctions and differences. Some are more or less in accordance with commonly accepted notions of equity, such as distinctions between skilled and unskilled workers, or appear to follow economic geography or to corrrespond with the profit position of employers. These we call differentials. Others exist without apparent reason. These we call inequities.[1] In still other situations with the soundest of economic bases for wage distinctions, none are to be found. Some differences persist indefinitely, others narrow gradually, and still others are eliminated entirely. The "national wage structure" seems to consist of little islands of rationality in a sea of anarchy.

Theoretical reconstruction must begin by the recognition of a few elementary facts. The trade union is a political instrumentality not governed by the pecuniary calculus conventionally attributed to business enterprise. (Others are better qualified to judge whether this is also true of the business enterprise itself.) The influences determining wages run in political more often than geographical or industrial orbits. Where a single price does emerge, there is established a prima facie case against the operation of market forces.

[1] One of the most engaging aspects of the National War Labor Board's eminently pragmatic program during the early years of World War II was the Board's capacity to distinguish between "historical differentials" and "gross inequities" without sacrificing the notion that it was administering the national wage structure evenhandedly and scientifically. Historical differentials had to be preserved; gross inequities had to be eliminated. In some cases, both themes were played simultaneously. For example, in *Chrysler Corporation,* the Board stated: "It should be pointed out that differences in rates are not necessarily inequalities in rates. On the contrary, the wages paid in American industry are normally characterized by all sorts of differentials created for many different reasons. Under any sound program for stabilizing wages in this time of war it must be presumed that well-established differences in wages are not inequalities. . . . One must not interpret the above-stated presumption, however, as an indication that established differences in wages can never become inequalities. They may be subject to adjustment if they have become inequalities which must be rectified in the interests of full production of war goods." Case No. 240, October 2, 1942, *War Labor Reports,* III: 451.

There are forces in society and in the economy making for uniformity in the wage structure, but they are not merely the forces of supply and demand. Ideas of equity and justice have long permeated industrial society, but the growth of organization has endowed them with compelling force. They provide the substance of equitable comparisons, and they govern the administration of consolidated bargaining structures. These are the strongest equalizing tendencies in wage determination.

Equitable comparisons are highly important to workers, employers, unions, and arbitrators. They attain additional strength through the administrative and political convenience of a ready-made settlement. They run in limited circuits, however, and not in a single chain throughout the whole economy. It is when the several locals of a single international union centralize their wage policies and consolidate their strategies, when separate industrial establishments are brought under common ownership, when the state plays an increasingly active role in setting rates of pay, when rival unions compete with one another for jurisdiction, when related unions negotiate together for mutual protection, and when employers organize into associations to preserve a common front that comparisons become coercive in the determination of wages. Under these circumstances small differences become large, and equal treatment becomes the *sine qua non* of industrial peace. A sixty-day strike over 2 cents an hour may be irrational in the economic lexicon, but viewed as political behavior it may have all the logic of survival.*

In a significant footnote on the effects of unionism in the interindustry field, Kerr notes there are really the following two questions regarding union influence on interindustry wages—questions which could be generalized to fit all structures. "(1) Has unionism been a source of comparative advantage to workers in unionized as contrasted with unorganized industries? and (2) Has unionism changed the pattern of relationship (narrowed the wage structure) among organized industries?" Kerr addresses his paper to the second of these questions.

However, he implies that in the interindustry structure, the failure of unionized industries to secure wage advantage over unorganized industries, as concluded in many statistical studies, indicates that unions have at least not been an element retarding the narrowing of the interindustry wage structure. Again at the interfirm level, Kerr

* Arthur M. Ross, *Trade Union Wage Policy* (University of California Press), pp. 72–74. Reprinted by permission of the author and publisher.

cites a study showing that wage dispersion among firms was lower in one city than in another less organized city as evidence that unions reduce interfirm differentials. In reality, the questions of union wage gain over nonunionized workers and union success in equalizing rates within the organized sector of labor markets are independent. Even if unions secured wage gains for heavily organized industries over nonunion industries, this would not prevent them from tending to equalize rates among the organized industries. Similarly, even if the interfirm differential were wider in an organized city than in an unorganized one, this would not mean that unions were not a force for wage equalization among the organized workers themselves; this would be the case if unions gained wide wage advantages for their members over nonunion rates. On the other hand, if the interindustry structure narrowed, as nonunion workers gained wage increases comparable to those of unionized workers, this would not necessarily indicate a narrowing of the differential within unionized industries, and if the interfirm differential narrowed, this need not necessarily mean that the wage differential narrowed among the unionized workers.

Thus, in appraising the influence of unions in standardizing rates, and in eliminating differentials among workers covered in wage agreements, it is illogical to study the changes in wage structures, which include union and nonunion workers, as a guide to the measurement of this influence. As a point of interest, there have been studies which question whether wage structure differentials are in the narrowing trend which Kerr describes. In any case, the trend of the structure differential is immaterial to the question of unions' contribution to the equalization of wage rates among union workers in particular labor markets.

The position at issue in Kerr's paper is the degree to which unions respond to membership pressure to standardize wage rates among covered workers within the same "orbit of coercive comparison" or what Dunlop would call, in his paper "The Task of Contemporary Wage Theory," also in *The Theory of Wage Determination*, on the same "wage contour." A more important question is whether unionism as an institution raises the level of wages. The concluding two papers concern themselves with this issue, the first of which supports the affirmative view that unionism has been an independent source of wage increases, and the second the negative view.

ROBERT OZANNE

Impact of Unions on Wage Trends and Income Distribution[*]

The following two selections reach conflicting conclusions on the role of unions in wage determination. While Robert Ozanne's research leads him to the view that unions are a strong force in raising wages, John E. Maher's analysis leads him to the opposite conclusion.

In appraising the influence of unions on wages, Ozanne adopts a new and daring approach. Dissatisfied with comparisons of wage gains between unionized and unorganized industries, because of their inability to isolate either the unionism variable or the influence of union wage changes on the unorganized sector, and the distributive shares method mainly because of its inclusion of employment as well as wage changes in the analysis, Ozanne uses what he calls the "period comparison method."

The first comparison is between wage levels during two time periods, the first in which production workers were but slightly unionized, the second in which they were mostly organized. Apart from the degree of unionization, movements in the major wage-determining economic variables, except prices, were similar during the two post-war periods studied. The effect of differential price changes was eliminated by a comparison of real wages. During the second (unionized) period, real wages of production workers rose at about twice the annual rate of the first (unorganized) period.

The second comparison is a modification of the distributive shares approach. Ozanne believes that the usual distributive shares procedure of considering the changing share of total national income for all employees—or, as implied in his paper, even for the production

[*] Reprinted by permission of the publishers from the *Quarterly Journal of Economics*, Volume LXXIII #2, May 1959 (Cambridge, Mass.: Harvard University Press). Copyright 1959 by The President and Fellows of Harvard College.

worker group—as a guide to union influence on income to be faulty because significant employment changes might obscure the effect of union wage pressure. If, as Ozanne contends, "the central objective of union bargaining . . . is to raise average member earnings, not to raise total employee income," then it would be obviously incorrect to evaluate the degree to which this objective was achieved by comparing the *total* share of income received by a group of workers before and after union wage pressure was exerted. By comparing changes in average annual income for particular groups during the two periods, this shortcoming of the usual distributive share approach is overcome.

Ozanne's approach can be considered novel because of its extension of the period comparison technique to the whole manufacturing sector, and more importantly because of its variant of the distributive share method of testing union influences on wages. Its boldness stems from its scope, its study of the manufacturing industries as a whole rather than of the individual industries within the group. Perhaps restrained by the breadth of coverage, at the cost of detail, Ozanne's conclusions are cautious and tentative. For example, "The data . . . all point toward unionism as a possible cause of the increased share of national income received by the average blue-collar worker in manufacturing . . ." and "The limited data here presented . . . seem perfectly consistent with an appreciable degree of trade union influence on income distribution."

I. INTRODUCTION

THERE is a widespread public belief as to the significant effect of unions on wage levels and income distribution. To date the academician has not found supporting evidence. Thus employers do not infrequently engage in knockdown battles with unions to escape the supposed squeeze of union wage demands. Workers by the millions make substantial investments in union dues in the firm belief that they are amply repaid by the resulting higher incomes. The Congress which passed the Taft-Hartley Act and numerous state legislatures are sold on the notion that union "monopolies" are a threat to public welfare. For the past three years the President of the United States in his *Economic Report* has, with increasing emphasis, warned unions against wage increases above productivity gains. Real wage rates continue their steady upward push despite the very substantial unemployment in certain industries in 1958.

In spite of all this, the bulk of professional academic opinion still seems to say that unions have little or no influence on wage levels and income distribution.

Clark Kerr holds,

[Trade unionism] can reduce labor's share through the furtherance of a policy of continuing full employment and perhaps also through the application of the standard rate. It can raise labor's share, in particular, through standard collective bargaining when employers cannot quickly escape; or through support of the application of effective price controls; or, in terms of kept income, through the encouragement of progressive taxation and subventions.

The other part of the answer is that, while it can raise labor's share, it cannot raise it by very much.[1]

According to John E. Maher,

This study of union-nonunion wage rate differentials leads to the conclusion that, for the industries and occupations considered, there are no significant differentials between the rates of workers in union and non-union plants.[2]

C. L. Christianson concludes,

. . . oligopolistic industries share no larger proportion of total income with employees because of the collective bargaining procedure than they would otherwise.[3]

Milton Friedman writes,

In a dynamic world, economic forces are always arising that tend to change relative wage rates. . . . In the absence of unions, these forces will operate more or less directly on wage rates. Given unions, the same forces will be present but they will operate indirectly on wage rates through the mediation of the union. . . . In many cases, so to speak, unions are simply thermometers registering the heat rather than furnaces producing the heat.[4]

[1] "Trade Unionism and Distributive Shares," American Economic Association, Papers and Proceedings, XLIV (May 1954), 279.
[2] "Union, Nonunion Wage Differentials," American Economic Review, XLVI (June 1956), 352.
[3] "Variations in the Inflationary Force of Bargaining," American Economic Association, Papers and Proceedings; XLIV (May 1954), 352.
[4] "Some Comments on the Significance of Labor Unions for Economic Policy," The Impact of the Union, ed. David McCord Wright (New York, 1951).

The above quotations at least imply that in so far as its effect on wage levels and income distribution is concerned, our elaborate collective bargaining process is little more than a superstitious ritual, resembling perhaps the fertility dances of primitive peoples. While public attention is diverted to the ritual, the traditional economic forces determine the results. In view of the dead seriousness with which unions and employers still practice this rite, it seems worthwhile to examine the problem further.

II. CRITICISMS OF EARLIER STUDIES

Effect of Unionism Too Small to Be Measured Until Recently

In terms of any economy-wide effect unions are too new to have had measurable effects prior to the post World War II period. Prior to the late 1930's unions were confined to the small percentage of workers in the skilled crafts. After 1937 union membership rose rapidly, but World War II blocked normal collective bargaining almost before it got started. Thus the War Labor Board restricted the bargaining power of the more highly paid unionized workers while granting large percentage increases to nonunion substandard wage groups. Not until 1946 did union bargaining in the mass production industries begin. Not only the studies of Douglas ending in 1926, but the more recent studies by Dunlop, Garbarino, Ross, and Levinson fail in point of time to catch the impact of post World War II union bargaining.

Wrong Emphasis on Distributive Shares

A second error of earlier studies has been the emphasis on distributive shares. This method is not precise enough for measuring the impact of unionism.

Of the 60 million persons listed by the Department of Commerce as "employees" only about one-fourth are members of unions. It is hardly reasonable to evaluate the bargaining impact of the 15 million unionists by changes in the income share of the entire 60 million employees, including office clerical employees, professionals, and corporate officers. Corporate officers are too few in number, so that their removal (as done by Levinson) cannot be expected to clarify the issue. Substantial influence by unions on the 15 million employees for whom they bargain might easily be submerged by the other 45 million.

Moreover the distributive share approach looks not at average income per employee, but at the total share income. If successful union bargaining substantially raised the average real income per employee at a time when technological changes reduced the total number of employees, total share income of employees might decline, thus concealing the effects of union bargaining. Likewise a 10 per cent rise in total share income due to an increase in the number of employees could not, by the distributive share approach, be differentiated from a 10 per cent rise in total share income due to an increase in average employee real earnings.

Other factors besides union bargaining affect the employee share. Some of these factors are: (1) changes in farm technology, which transfer farm entrepreneurs into urban employees and thus increase the labor share of national income; (2) increased industrial productivity which reduces the relative number of factory workers in the population and thus cuts the labor share; (3) degree of competition in the product market which may vary the profit and labor shares; (4) changes in consumer tastes which might raise the demand for non-employee services.

The distributive share approach does not permit segregation of the various factors influencing changes in the employee share. One of the refinements which can supplement the distributive share approach is the analysis of "average employee compensation" rather than "total employee compensation." It may then be possible to break down average employee compensation into those segments which are unionized and those which are not. Both of these refinements are attempted in the section of this paper entitled "Period Comparison Method."

Interindustry Comparison Method: Difficulty of Isolating Union Bargaining from Other Causes of Different Wage Paying Propensities of Different Industries

A third difficulty in studying the impact of unions has arisen from the shortcomings of the interindustry comparison method. This method, which avoids the distributive share approach, compares actual wage gains over a period of time between unionized and non-unionized industries.

The major shortcoming of this method is the inability to isolate unionism from other possible causes of wage changes. In contrast with classical theory the actual wages paid in different industries and firms appear to vary widely, even for the same quality of labor. Different industries for a variety of reasons appear to have differing propensities to pay and to raise wages. Thus a brewery may have a greater propensity to raise wages than a hosiery plant, a paper mill a greater propensity than a restaurant, a building contractor a greater propensity than a garment factory. Some of the possible causes of these differences apart from unionism may be: degree of public regulation, degree of price competition in the product market, market demand for labor, the desire of the employer to remain nonunionized, growth of the industry, profitability, the importance of public opinion to the employer, and the share which labor constitutes of the cost of production.

There have been several attempts to isolate possible causes of wage leadership. Dunlop by the simple correlation technique compared productivity and unionism as possible causes of wage gains in manufacturing industries. He concluded that productivity at least conditions the bargaining process and is more important than unionism.

Garbarino studied productivity, concentration of the industry, and unionism as possible causes of gains in average hourly earnings in manufacturing. He found both output per man hour and concentration were better indexes of wage gains than unionism. Concentration ranked slightly higher than productivity.

In neither of these studies was the correlation high enough to be conclusive. Both studies were limited to manufacturing. Unionism in the period studied (1923–40) was noticeably weak.

While these findings do not justify any conclusions, Garbarino's theoretical approach is interesting. He concludes that output per man hour is a "permissive" factor influencing wages and that concentration is a "positive" factor. It would be interesting to repeat Garbarino's study for the post World War II period and to include other sectors besides manufacturing. Had Garbarino included the building trades and the printing trades industries with above average wage increases and a low degree of concentration he might have contradicted his findings in manufacturing.

Douty, using Bureau of Labor Statistics data, compared union and nonunion wage rates for the same occupations in a wide variety of industries. He found that in 87 per cent of the occupations considered, wages of workers in unionized plants exceeded wages of workers in nonunionized plants. This is the most comprehensive of any of the studies. The advantage in favor of unions decreased some if the data were reviewed on a regional basis. There exists the possibility that if the unionized plants tend to be located in larger cities and nonunionized plants in small cities, Douty has to some extent merely compared wages in large cities with those in small cities.

Maher attempted to check Douty's omission by limiting his study to wage changes in unionized and nonunionized plants in the same geographical area. Thus any differences which may be found between unionized and nonunionized plants in the same industry would not be due to geography. Paint and varnish plants in Cleveland and footwear plants in a small New England area replace Douty's nation-wide comparisons. The selection of occupations eliminated sex difference and workers on incentive pay plans. Maher concluded that there were no significant differentials in unionized and non-unionized plants.

Maher's study pretty well isolated unionism from geographical and sex factors, but it failed to account for the influence of unionized plants over nearby nonunionized plants and vice versa. Furthermore it failed to observe what was the moving force in wage patterns. It may be that union influence is felt through wage pattern setting and that wages in nonunionized plants follow the lead of unions and differ only through time lags. Thus even though nonunionized plants kept up with the wages of unionized plants, the level of both may have been higher due to the pattern setting by the union.

Levinson combined the distributive share approach with the interindustry approach. He compared changes in the distributive shares received by a group of unionized industries on the one hand with those received by a group of nonunionized industries on the other. This method of study seems to combine the faults of both distributive share studies and interindustry comparisons.

As in the distributive share approach an increase in the labor share of the unionized sector might be due to either (a) a rise in the average wage per employee or (b) a rise in the number of employees. In looking at total employee income per share or per industry rather than average income per employee, the distributive share approach obliterates the central objective of union bargaining which is to raise average member earnings, not to raise total employee income. In addition, it lumps into one category white collar (generally non-union) and blue collar (generally union) employees, thus concealing any changed relationship between office and plant workers which may have occurred.

As with other interindustry comparisons, since industries have varying propensities to grant wage increases in response to identical union pressures, it is a serious error to attempt to evaluate the effect of unionism merely by measuring the size of the increase. In tunnel drilling the hardness of the rock varies. No one would attempt to measure the efficiency of different crews by measuring the length of the cut per work shift. Merely because a nonunionized industry made the same wage gain as a unionized industry does not enable us to conclude that the union had no effect. Comparing average gains of unionized and nonunionized industries does not give us any notion of what wages might be without a union.

A last difficulty in interindustry wage gain comparisons is the one of measurement. Should wage gains be measured in absolute cents per hour or as percentages over the base year? Is a 5 per cent (4¢ per hour) increase for the 80¢ variety store clerk to be equated with a 5 per cent (10¢ per hour) increase for the $2.00 an hour factory worker or the 5 per cent (15¢ per hour) increase for the $3.00 an hour building trades worker?

In some industries and situations it will take more bargaining power to get the 5 per cent increase for the $3.00 worker. In others the reverse will be true. Competitive conditions, the nature of the industry, the attitudes of employers, whether or not the settlement sets a new pattern, and the desire of the employer to avoid a union all have a bearing on whether or not equal percentage wage changes or equal absolute wage changes come closer to measuring the impact of unions in different conditions.

The pattern-setting union which pioneers a guaranteed annual wage or a new round of wage increases may need far more bargaining power than subsequent union and nonunion groups which merely follow the leader. A pattern-setting increase "softens" subsequent employers who were attempting to pay less and "stiffens" subsequent unions which might have accepted less.

At any rate the answers to the above questions may not be resolved so much by the abstract logic of the statistician as by measuring the bargaining force needed to move employers and employees under varying conditions. Simple wage comparisons in either percentage or absolute terms are not the final answer to this complex problem.

III. PERIOD COMPARISON METHOD

To avoid the pitfalls of interindustry comparisons, this study uses a period comparison method. In this method wage gains of an industry or group of industries in one period are compared with gains of the same industry or group in a different period. This method involves selecting two presumably comparable periods, one union and the other nonunion. Wage gains in each period are related to per capita income gains in each period.

Albert Rees used a simple version of this method to study union-nonunion wage behavior in the steel industry. He chose two inflationary periods. His nonunion period was 1914–20. The union period was 1939–48. He found that real earnings rose farther in the nonunion period. He concluded that unionism in steel in an inflationary period does not increase wages over what they would be without a union and that because of long-term contracts, unionism may actually restrain wage increases.

Rees's period comparison method has much to commend it. By comparing union and nonunion periods one can avoid the pervasive effect which unionized plant and industry wage policies have over nonunionized plant and industry wages.

If the periods are well selected one can observe wage behavior in identical industries under union and nonunion conditions. If the time interval between the two periods is not too long, the industry may exhibit many of the same characteristics, such as degree of competition in the product market, productivity, profitability, expansion of the industry, etc.

In Rees's study the periods chosen are probably too different for effective use of this "period comparison" technique. The bulk of the second period 1939–48 was characterized by rigid wage and price controls. Thus neither union bargaining power nor market demand for labor, nor market demand for a product in short supply were permitted to operate. Even the removal of price controls in 1946 was followed by the threat of price controls well through 1947. In the post World War II period the hostile government attitude toward price increases and the possible government operation of government-built steel mills forced the steel industry to sell its product far below the price called for by market conditions. The consequent effect on the company's wage policy invalidates any wage comparisons with the totally different conditions from 1918 to 1920. Moreover, as Sumner Slichter has pointed out, 1918 and 1919 can hardly be classified as a nonunion period. It witnessed the greatest proportion of workers ever to go on strike, including a highly successful union organizing drive in steel and a strike which closed down the bulk of the steel industry.

Nevertheless, the period comparison method used here by Rees has much to commend it. With more carefully selected time periods it avoids most of the difficulties of the interindustry comparison method.

The periods chosen for this study are the prosperous periods after both world wars, 1923–29 and 1947–57. The post World War I period is the six year period, 1923–29. For the post World War II period as much of the ten year period as possible is used. In some cases wage data are available through 1957, in some cases only through 1955, and productivity data are available only through 1953.

In spite of some differences the two periods are surprisingly similar. Tables I through IV give economic data on the two periods.

TABLE I — PER CAPITA PERSONAL INCOME GAIN PER YEAR, REAL DOLLARS

Period	Per capita personal income gain per year[1]
	%
Post World War I, 1923–29[2]	1.74
Post World War II, 1947–57[3]	2.08

1 Based on compound interest formula.
2 National Industrial Conference Board, *The Economic Almanac, 1951–52*, p. 210.
3 U. S. Congress, Joint Economic Committee, *Economic Indicators*, Sept. 1958, p. 4.

In terms of the growth of the economy, Table I demonstrates that the rate of growth in the two periods was reasonably similar.

TABLE II — GAIN IN PHYSICAL OUTPUT PER MAN HOUR IN MANUFACTURING

Period	Gain in physical output per man hour per year, manufacturing[1]
	%
Post World War I, 1923–29[2]	4.64
Post World War II, 1947–53[3]	3.45

1 Based on compound interest formula.
2 U. S. Department of Labor, *Handbook of Labor Statistics*, 1950, p. 168.
3 *Trends in Output Per Man Hour and Man Hours Per Unit Output, Manufacturing, 1939–53*, Bureau of Labor Statistics Report No. 100, p. 315.

Table II above shows productivity somewhat ahead in the post World War I period. While productivity figures are not as precise in their meaning as many of our more common statistics, the figures of Table II indicate clearly that the economy in the post World War I period was certainly not less able to support wage increases than in the post World War II period.

The greatest difference in the periods is to be found in price behavior.

The post World War I period was one of relative price stability. The later period was characterized through 1951 by substantial price

TABLE III — CONSUMER PRICES[1]

Period	Annual rate of increase[2]
	%
Post World War I, 1923–29	.09
Post World War II, 1947–57	2.36

1 Bureau of Labor Statistics consumer price index from *Economic Indicators.*
2 Based on compound interest formula.

increases. Since wages have a tendency to lag behind price increases the post World War I period was more conducive to real wage increases, especially since in the real increase in per capita income and in productivity, Period I was every bit the equal of Period II.

TABLE IV — UNEMPLOYMENT AS A PERCENTAGE OF THE LABOR FORCE

Period	Unemployment as a percentage of the labor force, annual average
Post World War I, 1923–29	2.9[1] (est.)
Post World War II, 1947–57	4.3[2]

1 Woytinsky, *Employment and Wages in the United States,* p. 397.
2 Bureau of Labor Statistics data as reported in *Economic Indicators.*

No accurate figures on unemployment were kept in the twenties, and the estimate of unemployment is probably too conservative. But these figures, plus the very considerable farm-city migration in both periods, indicate that in neither period was there a tight over-all labor market. The brief exception would be during the Korean crisis. Here no real shortage of labor developed, but late in 1950 employers did some hoarding of workers in anticipation of a shortage which never developed because of the short duration and limited nature of the Korean War.

While the expanded role of government in the post World War II period as compared with the period of the twenties is often referred to as a major difference, in its economic effects the role of government is exaggerated. In 1929 government accounted for 6 per cent of the nation's total gross national product. In 1946 the government sector had increased to only 10 per cent. Since most of this increase occurred from 1941 to 1945, there is no reason to believe that government activity had a significant effect on the wage patterns of the nation. The exception, again, occurred during the Korean War, when government expenditures for war supplies had an inflationary effect on wages. Since at this time (1950–51) prices rose as fast as wages, the net effect of government expenditures plus government wage controls was to hold down real wages. Except for a few months in late 1950, wage behavior during the Korean War does not appear to have differed fundamentally from the rest of the post World War II period.

In summary, the two periods bear significant resemblances. At least in their wage paying abilities as measured by productivity and national income growth, neither period seems to have much advantage over the other.

IV. WAGE BEHAVIOR IN NONUNION (1923–29) AND UNION (1947–55) PERIODS

The first comparison of wage gains on the period basis is that for manufacturing, which has the advantage of including many industries and a very large segment of wage earners. In 1929 production workers in manufacturing were only 11 per cent unionized, as compared with 67 per cent in 1956.

The hypothesis we are testing is that the greatly increased proportion of union members in the post World War II period has substantially altered wage patterns from those found in the nonunion twenties, and further, that this altered wage pattern has given the average hourly wage earner in manufacturing a greater share of national income than he received in the twenties. To what extent do available data support the above hypothesis?

Table V lists the current average hourly earnings of manufacturing workers in the two periods.

Table V reveals a phenomenal change in the wage patterns of the two periods. In the twenties wages remained stationary year after year. In the post World War II period wages moved upward year after year. Since the characteristic of union wage bargaining is to negotiate for annual wage increments, unions are eligible for serious consideration as probable causes of the changed pattern. The twenties with its long period of wage stability appears to be characteristic of wages in a nonunion period.

Are the wage increases of the union period illusory or real — Table VI converts the data into real terms.

As Table VI shows, the regular annual increments negotiated by unions are real and substantial. Since they occur in years of stable prices as well as in years of price increases they cannot be attributed

TABLE V — AVERAGE HOURLY EARNINGS OF PRODUCTION WORKERS IN
MANUFACTURING, CURRENT PRICES[1]

Nonunion period		Union period	
	Average hourly earnings		
1923	$.52	$1.24	1947
1924	.55	1.35	1948
1925	.55	1.40	1949
1926	.55	1.47	1950
1927	.55	1.59	1951
1928	.56	1.67	1952
1929	.57	1.77	1953
		1.81	1954
		1.88	1955
		1.98	1956
		2.07	1957
annual rate of increase[2]	1.54%	5.24%	

1 *Historical and Descriptive Supplement to Economic Indicators,* 1955, p. 29, and *Economic Indicators,* Mar. 1958.
2 Based on compound interest formula.

TABLE VI — AVERAGE HOURLY EARNINGS IN REAL DOLLARS FOR PRODUC-
TION WORKERS IN MANUFACTURING, 1923–1929 AND 1947–
1957 (CONSTANT PRICES)[1]

Post World War I period		Post World War II period	
	Average hourly earnings in real dollars		
1923	$.82	$1.51	1947
1924	.86	1.53	1948
1925	.84	1.60	1949
1926	.83	1.66	1950
1927	.85	1.66	1951
1928	.88	1.71	1952
1929	.89	1.80	1953
		1.83	1954
		1.92	1955
		1.98	1956
		2.00	1957
annual rate of increase[2]	1.375%	2.80%	

1 *Historical and Descriptive Supplement to Economic Indicators,* 1955, p. 29, 1957,
p. 31, and *Economic Indicators,* Mar. 1958.
2 Based on compound interest formula.

to the effects of inflation. If accurate data on fringe benefits were readily available, the rate of increase in the union period would average somewhat higher.

What is the gain in production workers' income compared with that of other groups in the two periods? Tables VIIa and VIIb give comparisons with other groups.

Tables VIIa and VIIb lead to some very important conclusions:

(1) Average income per full-time employee lagged behind increases in per capita personal income in the nonunion period, but did substantially better than per capita personal income gains in the union period. This supports the probability that gains which went to union workers were not made at the expense of nonunion employees. All employees (No. 2, Table VIIa) in the union period received larger average wage increases in relation to per capita personal income gains than in the nonunion period.

TABLE VIIa — PERCENTAGE COMPARISONS OF GAINS IN AVERAGE ANNUAL INCOME[1]

	Nonunion period 1923–29 (6 years)	Union period 1947–55 (8 years)
(1) Gain in average annual per capita personal income	100[2]	100[3]
(2) Gain in average annual compensation per full-time employee (all industries)	71[4]	134[5]
(3) Gain in average annual income per white collar worker in manufacturing	157[6]	143[7]
(4) Gain in average annual income per production worker in manufacturing	42[6]	144[7]

1 Figures are expressed as a per cent of gain in per capita income, constant dollars.
2 *Economic Almanac, 1951–52,* p. 210.
3 *Economic Report of the President,* 1957, p. 104.
4 Simon Kuznets, *National Income and Its Composition, 1919–1938,* pp. 314–15.
5 *National Income Supplement to the Survey of Current Business, 1954,* p. 201. *Survey of Current Business,* July 1957, table 27.
6 *Statistical Abstract of the United States,* 1956, p. 791.
7 U. S. Department of Commerce, *Annual Survey of Manufactures.*

(2) White collar workers in manufacturing (No. 3, Table VIIa) who fared so well in the nonunion twenties were keeping well ahead of per capita personal incomes in the union period, although they had a better relative position in the twenties.

TABLE VIIb — GAINS IN AVERAGE ANNUAL INCOME[1]

	Nonunion period 1923–29 (6 years)	Union period 1947–55 (8 years)
	%	%
(1) Gain in average annual per capita personal income	1.74	1.98
(2) Gain in average annual compensation per full-time employee (all industries)	1.23	2.66
(3) Gain in average annual income per white collar worker in manufacturing	2.74	2.83
(4) Gain in average annual income per production worker in manufacturing	.73	2.85

1 Table VIIa was constructed from these data. The sources are the same as those for Table VIIa. Figures are expressed as an annual rate of increase, based on constant dollars and a compound interest formula.

(3) Production workers in manufacturing (No. 4, Table VIIa) showed the most striking gains. In the nonunion twenties the stable wage pattern set by employers left them far behind gains of the population generally, as measured by per capita personal incomes. In the union period the union-established wage pattern of regular annual increases pulled production workers well ahead of per capita income gains and gave them gains equal to those of white collar workers in the same industries.

These conclusions might be said to lend considerable weight to the hypothesis that unions have so changed the wage pattern in American industry that not only are production workers in manufacturing substantially better off relative to per capita personal income, but that all employees as a group, nonunion as well as union, are receiving relatively better annual incomes.

This type of time period comparison has certain advantages over the union-nonunion industry comparison method. The time period method establishes for each time period a benchmark such as per capita personal income against which income behavior of other groups may be measured.

When comparing income gains of one or more groups in different periods the annual rates of gain as shown in Table VIIb, Nos. 2, 3, and 4 are not particularly significant. These rates of gain must first be related to the average gain of the entire population in the period under consideration.

Table VIIa gives this relationship. The important consideration is not whether production workers gained at a higher rate in one period than in another, but how production workers' gains ranked in each period in relation to gains of other groups. Per capita personal income has been used as the benchmark in each period.[5] Thus, white collar workers' incomes went up faster in the 1947–55 period than in the twenties (No. 3, Table VIIb). But relative to the gains of other groups, white collar workers did better in the twenties (No. 3, Table VIIa). We are here concerned more with relative gains in income captured by various groups in both periods than with whether a group's income rose faster in one period than in the other. Presumably union bargaining might have influenced the relative status of production workers in manufacturing from the twenties to the post World War II period (No. 4, Table VIIa).

The data in Tables V through VIIb all point toward unionism as a possible cause of the increased share of national income received by the average blue collar worker in manufacturing in the 1947–55 period as compared with his share in the 1923–29 period.

We now, in Table VIII, look at wage gains for both periods in industries other than manufacturing for which wage data are available. These industries — railroads, bituminous coal mining, printing and construction — unlike manufacturing were substantially influenced by unions in the 1923–29 period.

With the exception of building construction, each of the industrial groups in Table VIII showed greater relative gain in the 1947–55 period than in the 1923–29 period. As indicated in Table VIII all groups were much more highly unionized in the later period. Wage gains (except in building construction) coincide with unionization.

Bituminous coal mining is a special case but in it, as in railroads and printing, wage gains correspond with the degree of unionization. The percentage of unionization in coal mining fell from 57 in 1923 to 37 in 1929. The disintegration of the union was accompanied by actual wage cuts of 20 per cent in average hourly rates. It is true that use of substitute fuels and a declining market for coal accom-

---

[5] There are logically as many reasons for using per capita national income as a benchmark as there are for using per capita personal income. Actually in these two periods the two indices moved so closely that substituting per capita national income for per capita personal income would not noticeably change the results.

panied this wage decline. Yet the industry suffered greater contraction in the 1947–55 period while wages of an almost 100 per cent unionized work force rose 32 per cent per hour plus substantial gains in fringe benefits.

TABLE VIII — GAINS OF WAGE EARNERS AND PERCENTAGE OF UNIONIZATION IN MANUFACTURING AND INDUSTRY

	1923–29		1947–55	
	income gain	percentage unionized 1929[1]	income gain	percentage unionized 1946[2]
Per capita personal income[3]	100		100	
Average hourly earnings:				
Class I railroads[4]	93	44.6	197	80–100
Bituminous coal[4]	negative	37.4	170	80–100
Printing[4]	148[5]	63(1930)	179	80–100
Building construction[4]	231[5]	26.7	215	80–100
Manufacturing (production workers)[4]	79[6]	10.9	141	67[7]

1 Leo Wolman, *op. cit.*, pp. 199, 204, 213–16, 227, 229–31.

2 *Extent of Collective Bargaining and Union Recognition, 1946*, Bureau of Labor Statistics, Bulletin No. 909.

3 *The Economic Almanac, 1951–52*, p. 210; *Economic Indicators*.

4 *Handbook of Labor Statistics*, 1950; Harold H. Levinson, *Unionism, Wage Trends and Income Distribution, 1914–47*, p. 34; *Statistical Abstract of the United States*, 1957, p. 225; *Monthly Labor Review*, June 1956, p. 726.

5 Union wage rates.

6 The reason that production workers in manufacturing from 1923–29 gained more in Table VIII than in Table VIIa is because Table VIII measures average hourly earnings, while Table VIIa measures annual earnings. From 1923–29 the work week was cut approximately 3 per cent so that annual income was likewise cut. If annual earnings in Table VIIa were projected on the basis of the same weekly hours worked in 1929 as in 1923 the two tables would be almost identical. Table VIIa, expressed in average annual earnings, therefore understates earnings of production workers to the extent that some of their gains were taken in leisure.

7 Data from *Monthly Labor Review*, Oct. 1957, pp. 1208 and 1270.

The building trades case appears to refute the others. Here the more highly organized building trades of the 1947–55 period did not do quite as well relative to per capita income gains as in the 1923–29 period. There are a number of possible explanations. First, the unreliability of the figures may overstate the gains of the building trades in the twenties. As Table IX states, wage figures for the building trades, 1923–29, are union wage scales, not actual average hourly earnings. Union wage scales of the 1923–29 period are limited to the large cities. Hence in building construction we are comparing the large city wage gains of 1923–29 with all area wage gains in 1947–55.

Perhaps the percentage of the total trade organized is not always a good index of bargaining strength. Building construction is a local industry. A powerful building trades union in a large city during the twenties may not have been hindered by the sea of nonunion areas surrounding it. The good relative showing of wages in building construction in the twenties is consistent with strong union influence confined to the big cities.

The building boom of the twenties no doubt helps explain the reason building construction wages rose more than wages for other groups in the same period, but it does not explain why they exceeded relative building construction wage gains in the 1947–55 period. As Table IX indicates, market demand for construction labor was as high in the 1947–55 period as from 1923–29.

Table VIII reveals that the workers in the partially unionized industries (except building construction) of the twenties improved their positions as their degree of unionization rose in the 1947–55 period. These findings are consistent with the findings from the examination of wage gains in manufacturing as shown in Tables V through VIIa.

V. COLLECTIVE BARGAINING VS. MARKET DEMAND IN UNION AND NONUNION PERIODS

To what extent might the wage advantages of the union period revealed in Table VIII be accounted for by market demand for labor rather than by union bargaining strength? Table IX below casts serious doubt on the influence of market demand.

Table IX demonstrates a significant shift in the relation between wage behavior and market demand for labor from the nonunion twenties to the union post World War II period. In the twenties wages behaved about as expected in accordance with market demand theory. The major exception might be the railroad industry, which being partially unionized in the twenties, was able to counteract the forces of the market. In the post World War II period wage behavior appears to have overcome market demand as an important causal factor. What has apparently happened in the 1947–55 period is that a more powerful force, collective bargaining, has dwarfed and all but obliterated the evidence of market forces. Of course, market pressures still exist. Witness the difference between the auto negotiations of 1955 and 1958. The resultant wage in the union period is

TABLE IX — COMPARISON OF WAGE AND EMPLOYMENT CHANGES IN
UNION AND NONUNION PERIODS[1]

	Nonunion period (1923–29)		Union period (1947–55)	
	employment changes	wage changes	employment changes	wage changes
Manufacturing:[2]	%	%	%	%
Production workers	.36	.73	.83	2.85
Nonproduction workers (white collar)	.14	2.74	3.92	2.83
Bituminous coal production workers[3]	−5.47	−3.62	−9.08	3.37
Class I railroad workers[4]	−1.78	1.61	−3.03	3.90
Building construction workers[5]	3.63	4.23	3.30	4.26
Printing trades workers[6]	—	2.72	.803	3.55

1 Figures are expressed as an annual rate of increase based on a compound interest formula. Wage figures are in constant dollars.
2 Based on data from *Statistical Abstract of the United States*, 1958, p. 774, adjusted for comparability. Wages are annual incomes; employment is average annual.
3 Based on data from *Historical Statistics of the United States, 1789–1945*, Bureau of the Census, p. 143; *Handbook of Labor Statistics*, 1950, p. 56; *Monthly Labor Review*, Nov. 1956, pp. 1336 and 1349. Wages are average hourly earnings.
4 Data from Bureau of Labor Statistics, *Trend of Employment and Labor Turnover*, Nov. 1923, p. 25; Bureau of Labor Statistics, Bulletin No. 1016, pp. 25, 76 and 83; *Monthly Labor Review*, Nov. 1956; pp. 1339 and 1363. Wages are average hourly earnings.
5 Based on data from *Handbook of Labor Statistics*, 1950, pp. 5, 57 and 89; *Monthly Labor Review*, June 1956, pp. 712 and 726. Employment figures for construction are based on Bureau of Labor Statistics index of contract construction which includes more than just building construction. Wages for 1923–29 are union wage scales. Wages for 1947–55 are average hourly earnings.
6 Based on data from *Handbook of Labor Statistics*, 1950, pp. 9, 204; *Statistical Abstract of the United States*, 1957, pp. 204, 255; Harold H. Levinson, *Unionism, Wage Trends and Income Distribution, 1914–47, op. cit.*, p. 34. Wages are average hourly earnings.

a compromise between the two pressures. It would appear from the data in Table IX that collective bargaining is the more potent force.

VI. INCIDENCE OF WAGE GAINS

If production workers were doing relatively better in the union post World War II period, it follows that some one or more of the income recipients must have been relatively less well off than in the twenties. Who were they? Tables Xa and Xb showing distributive share changes in the two periods throw some light on this question.

While profits during the union period have held their own in comparison with national income, they have failed to make the relative advance which they made in the nonunion period. Rent and unincorporated income were actual losers. While employee compensation fared better in the union period, referral to Table VIIa indicates that all the gains in the 1947–55 period went to the blue collar group.

TABLE Xa — COMPARISON OF INCOME GAINS BY DISTRIBUTIVE SHARES, UNION AND NONUNION PERIODS[1]

	Income gains as a percentage of national income gain (constant dollars)	
	Nonunion period 1923–29	Union period 1947–56
National income, unadjusted	100.0	100.0
Employee compensation	100.7	129.5
Corporate profits before taxes (adjusted for inventory changes)	176.5[2]	106.9[2]
Corporate profits before taxes (unadjusted)	182.4	57.1
Interest	157.3	286.6
Rent	131.6	61.7
Unincorporated enterprise income (adjusted)		21.4[2]
Business and professional	72.6[2]	62.7[2]

[1] Simon Kuznets, *National Income and Its Composition, 1919–1938*, pp. 310–19, 900. *Survey of Current Business*, July 1957, p. 16.
[2] Adjusted national income figures used.

TABLE Xb — COMPARISON OF INCOME GAINS BY DISTRIBUTIVE SHARES, UNION AND NONUNION PERIODS[1]

	Income gain as an annual rate of increase[2] (constant dollars)	
	Nonunion period 1923–29	Union period 1947–56
National income, unadjusted	3.07	3.73
Employee compensation	3.09	4.83
Corporate profits before taxes (adjusted for inventory changes)	5.42	3.99
Corporate profits before taxes (unadjusted)	5.60	2.13
Interest	4.83	10.69
Rent	4.04	2.30
Unincorporated enterprise income (adjusted)		−.08
Business and professional	2.23	2.34

[1] Sources same as for Table Xa.
[2] Based on compound interest formula.

The fact that "employee compensation" gained substantially during the prosperous years 1947–56 should raise serious doubts about the often expressed notion that the labor share remains constant. Profits are notoriously volatile. In the short run it is hazardous to draw any conclusions about them. They may even have been understated in the post Korean War period due to rapid write-offs of new plant and accelerated depreciation permitted by the tax laws of 1954.

VII. CONCLUSION

The following comparisons between the nonunion period, 1923–29, and the union post World War II period beginning in 1947 are consistent with substantial trade union collective bargaining impact on income distribution:

(1) Real average hourly earnings of production workers in manufacturing in the union period rose over twice as rapidly as in the nonunion period (Table VI), although increase in productivity in manufacturing as measured by change in physical output per man hour was greater in the nonunion period (Table II).

(2) Average annual compensation per full-time employee (all industries) rose less than per capita personal income in the nonunion period but exceeded gains in per capita personal income in the union period (Tables VIIa and VIIb).

(3) The rate of increase in average annual incomes of white collar workers in manufacturing far outdistanced that of production workers in the same industries in the nonunion period. In the union period the rate of increase in average annual incomes of production workers slightly exceeded that of white collar workers (Tables VIIa and VIIb).

(4) In the nonunion period the rate of increase in average annual incomes of production workers lagged well behind the rate of increase in per capita personal income. In the union period the situation was reversed (Tables VIIa and VIIb). Average hourly earnings of production workers in manufacturing showed the same trends (Table VIII).

(5) Three out of four groups which were partially organized in the twenties showed greater relative gain in the 1947–55 period as their degree of unionization rose to nearly 100 per cent. (Bituminous coal, Class I railroads, and printing, Table VIII). Building construction, on the contrary, showed greater relative gains in the twenties with a lower degree of unionization than in the 1947–55 period. But the fact that building construction wage data of the twenties were

confined to union wage scales in large cities casts doubt on findings as they relate to building construction.

(6) Wage movements in the union period show surprising independence of market demand for labor (Table IX).

(7) The distributive share of employees remained constant in the nonunion period. It rose in the union period (Table X).

(8) The distributive share of profits before taxes (adjusted for inventory changes) rose in the nonunion period and remained relatively stable in the union period (Table X).

The period comparison method will never provide "proof" of anything since the number of periods under observation is always too few to eliminate what the statistician calls "random fluctuations." The limited data here presented, however, seem perfectly consistent with an appreciable degree of trade union influence on income distribution.

If data on 1958 had been included the result would have been to accentuate the role of unions. This is because in 1958 profits dove while wage rates either held their own or continued their upward trend. For unions to maintain the relative income position of workers in the face of simultaneous unemployment and inflation is indeed evidence of some kind of evolutionary change.

To make a prediction, I would suggest that the accumulating bulk of evidence gathered since 1947 will support the notion of businessmen, politicians, and trade unionists — that collective bargaining is more than a ritual.

COMMENT

In dealing with summary data of a large number of individual items, there is always the risk that changes in the total figures might merely reflect internal shifts among the items rather than movements in the items themselves. Referring to Ozanne's study, the apparent gain in the blue-collar wage rate might have resulted mainly not from higher wage rates but from the relative growth in employment in the high wage industries (aircraft and automobiles, for example) and relative decline in low wage industries (textiles and apparel, for example). Had this been the case, a search for factors that increased wage rates would have been a waste of time. However, a study of the wage changes for manufacturing industries, for which data were available for the two periods, with 1923–1929 industry employment as weights, would show that the change in the industry mix was an insignificant element in the rise in average wage levels for the manufacturing sector as a whole.

A more controversial issue is Ozanne's use of average rather than total wage or income data in evaluating union influence through changes in relative share in order to isolate wage and income changes per worker from employment changes. Implied in this method is the view that unions are predominantly wage conscious and not employment conscious. Many economists share this view. Ross for example, in *Trade Union Wage Policy*, claims unions are not employment conscious because the employment effects of a wage increase are too uncertain. Lester's evidence, presented earlier, was that employers considered wages an unimportant (short-run) determinant of employment.

On the other hand there is evidence and authority to support the view that unions are concerned about the employment effects of their wage demands, especially during depressions. Presumably, though Ozanne's union period was a prosperous one, employment would have been greater or jobs easier to find had unions pressed less for higher wages.

Assume for the moment that Ozanne's view is the wrong one, and that unions are at least just as interested in employment as wage rate movements. Then, the average income comparisons would be the wrong ones for testing whether unions achieved their economic objectives. But the issue of Ozanne's paper, and of this section, is not whether unions get what they want but whether they exert an upward force on wages. Thus, whatever the importance unions attach to employment effects, average income changes are the correct measurement for examining the influence of unions on wages.

The use of this method is not a refinement of the shares approach but its abandonment. Nevertheless, Ozanne appears to reintroduce it in Table X. The gain in the share of national income of employee compensation during the union period is associated with the blue-collar group wage gain. However, the share measurement is of total income values, not average, and also includes employment changes. Thus the blue-collar share gain, considering the relative decline in blue-collar employment, was much less than its relative average income gain. In any case, Table X is not central to Ozanne's thesis.

There is a tacit acceptance of the "sympathetic pressure" notion in Ozanne's explanation that the gains secured by the (unionized) blue-collar workers might have been a factor raising wages throughout the employee group. There is some doubt concerning the strength of sympathetic pressure even on nonunion production worker wages. Certainly the pressure is weaker on such dissimilar work as is found in many white-collar job classifications. To attribute the strong gain in relative wages among the white-collar workers to a reaction to wage increases among the unionized blue-collar workers requires a great deal of substantiation.

Ozanne points out the uncertainty in the correct measurement of wage or income changes, whether on an absolute or percentage basis. However, he uses the percentage method uncritically in comparing blue-collar and white-collar income. The almost equal percentage gain of the two groups represents a much higher absolute wage gain for the higher paid white-collar workers during the union period.

JOHN E. MAHER

Union, Nonunion Wage Differentials*

While the preceding selection by Robert Ozanne studied the effect of unionism on wages as a whole, Maher's article presents an example of the microeconomic approach to the question of union influence on wages. Every effort is made to isolate the unionism variable from other wage-determining elements. Union-nonunion time wage rate comparisons are made of workers in the same occupation within the same metropolitan area in plants of approximately the same size. Applying a variety of statistical tests, the limited scope of the study allows for close statistical scrutiny.

* Reprinted by permission of the author from the *American Economic Review*, XLVI (June 1956), 336–352.

Maher hypothesizes that at equilibrium, "there are no significant differences in the wage rates of workers in union and nonunion plants." Aware of the fact that any static study of wage rates at a point in time is subject to the influence of dynamic disequilibrating forces, Maher suggests that the union-nonunion differential is more apt to be insignificant during stable periods. In fact, Maher attributes the differential that exists in furniture (in favor of the union workers) and in footwear (in favor of nonunion workers) to the timing of his wage data. He infers that if the wage surveys that served for his statistical studies of these two industries had been made later, when the effects of union wage agreements had had sufficient time to be felt throughout the industries, the union-nonunion wage differential would have been as insignificant in them as in the other industries, surveyed during their stable periods.

THE study presented in the following pages is an attempt to improve the state of knowledge with respect to the existence and significance of the wage advantage attributed by many economists to union workers over their unorganized counterparts. For although it is obvious that unions are frequently negotiating wage increases for their constituents, it is by no means apparent that these wage gains are (1) greater than these constituents would have received had the establishments in which they are employed never been organized nor (2) greater than nonunion workers are receiving without benefit of union representation.[1] It is to an assessment of the second and simpler of these two possibilities that the attention of the present research is directed. That is, we seek to discover from carefully selected data whether or not workers in unionized plants possess a significant wage advantage over workers in similar but nonunionized plants.[2]

[1] It is true, of course, that nonunion workers may derive the same benefits as union workers because of the pervasive influence of unionism upon the economy as a whole. For a forceful presentation of this view see S. H. Slichter, "Do the Wage-Fixing Arrangements in the American Labor Market Have an Inflationary Bias?," Am. Econ. Rev., Proceedings, May 1954, XLIV, 322–46.

[2] For a more detailed treatment, reference is made to the author's doctoral dissertation, "Union, Nonunion Wage Rate Differentials," (Harvard University, 1954). J. T. Dunlop provided the initial stimulus and continued encouragement for this investigation. Although the wage data for the empirical part of this research were obtained while the author was employed by the Bureau of Labor Statistics, the Bureau cannot be associated with the validity of the findings.

Many attacks upon this problem of measuring union, nonunion wage differentials have been made since Paul H. Douglas' classic study, *Real Wages in the United States 1800–1926.* The methodology employed has consisted of dividing workers whose wages were to be analyzed into two groups, those employed in industries substantially organized by unions and those in industries not so organized. Average hourly earnings series were selected to represent the wage movements for each group and comparisons were made between the changes in earnings among industries over time. Some of the investigators have concluded that the influence of unions has resulted in greater wage rises in organized than in unorganized industries; another, that the opposite result has occurred, namely, that nonunion workers have secured greater wage gains; while others believe that unionism has exerted either no significant influence or an ambiguous influence upon wage movements. Some of the apparent contradictions in these findings may be due to the fact that these studies differ in the time periods considered, the industries represented, and so on. It is more pertinent, however, that the investigations employed a highly unreliable measure of wages and, furthermore, that even had measurement been precise, the problem of the explanation of interindustry wage movements is too fraught with complexities for fruitful results to be obtained from so cursory a treatment.

It is the price of labor per unit of time that must be measured in ascertaining the influence of unionism on wages; but changes in average hourly earnings are usually poor measures of changes in the price of labor because of discrepancies in variations between the two.[3] Indeed, Reynolds has questioned whether average hourly earnings ". . . really measures anything which is statistically precise or theoretically interesting."[4] However, even if these aggregative approaches had been precise in measurement, it is doubtful if the differential movements in earnings revealed by them could be attributed to union-

---

[3] My doctoral dissertation, previously cited, develops empirical verification for this conclusion: *op cit.,* pp. 33–39. Changes in the following factors will, *ceteris paribus,* cause changes in earnings while basic wage rates remain unchanged: overtime and other premium rates, shift differentials, and proportions of workers employed at higher and lower rates. Similar effects flow from changes in the proportions of large and small plants in the sample, shifts in the geographical distribution of plants and changes in the skill, age and sex composition of the work forces. *Cf.* J. T. Dunlop, *Wage Determination under Trade Unions* (New York, 1950), pp. 19–27.

[4] L. G. Reynolds, "Economics of Labor," *A Survey of Contemporary Economics,* Vol. I, ed. H. S. Ellis (Philadelphia, 1948), p. 262.

ism because of the intrusion of so many uncontrolled variables, such
as interindustry changes in quantities and efficiencies of productive
factors and in the structures of markets. Thus the comparison of
changes in earnings is too imprecise and fails to isolate the crucial
variable, unionism.[5]

The following discussion of a different approach to the problem
is divided into four sections. Section I presents the new approach;
Section II is devoted to an appraisal of the statistical significance of
the wage rate differentials that have been discovered. An explanation
of these differentials is offered in Section III, and general conclusions
are presented in Section IV.

I. A MICROECONOMIC APPROACH TO THE PROBLEM

The method of the present study has been to compare average wage
rates of union and nonunion workers in the same industry, occupation, geographic area and employed in plants of the same size. Since
rates, not earnings, were to be compared, incentive workers were excluded from consideration: their average hourly earnings are the only
available measures of their rates and these measures are considered
unreliable. Data for an investigation of 7 industries were secured
from the 1950 industry-locality studies of the Bureau of Labor Statistics. These industries are paints and varnishes, furniture (wooden,
other than upholstered), footwear (men's Goodyear welt and women's
cement process), cotton textiles, hosiery (full-fashioned, men's seamless and children's seamless), automotive parts (engine and chassis)
and women's dresses.[6] A preliminary task was the definition and
selection of comparable union and nonunion plants within each of
the industries. A union plant is defined by the Bureau as one in

5 Even if studies of this kind had been able to demonstrate statistically significant interindustry wage differentials attributable to unionism, it would not
necessarily follow that economically significant differentials had been discovered — that is, differentials which indicate "distortions" of the wage structure.
For this to hold, it must be true that a more nearly optimal allocation of labor
would prevail in the absence of unions and that there were no hindrances to
the movement of labor (other than unions) in the form of costs of movement
or inadequacy of knowledge of alternative employments. Cf. A. C. Pigou, The
Economics of Welfare, 2nd ed. (London, 1924), pp. 470–76.

6 Classifications are those of the standard industrial classification system. The
specifications in parentheses indicate the extent to which product distinctions
were possible. Details on the method of collecting wage rate data together with
descriptions of concepts used are found in Wages Studies Manual of Procedure,
BLS, Washington, Nov. 1951. The data on which the present study is based
have not been published. However, they are included in the Bureau's published

which at least 50 per cent of the workers are covered by the terms of collective bargaining agreements. The criteria for comparability of plants were proximity and size as measured by number of employees. To insure geographical proximity, plants were held comparable only if located in the same metropolitan area. Plants were considered comparable in size if they fell within the same class interval in a frequency distribution of plants by number of workers employed.

Table I presents the coverage of the data used in the present study in relation to the universes from which they were drawn. From universes of more than 200,000 workers, wage rates for over 11,000 have been selected; the sample size thus exceeds 5 per cent.

TABLE I — COVERAGE OF WAGE DATA FOR 7 INDUSTRIES BY NUMBER OF PLANTS AND NUMBER OF EMPLOYEES IN THE UNIVERSE AND IN THE PRESENT STUDY

	Universe		Present study[1]							
			Plants				Employees			
Industry	No. of plants[2]	No. of employees	Total	Per cent of universe	Union	Nonunion	Total No.	Per cent of universe	Tabulated number	Per cent of universe
I. Paints and varnishes	460	19,993	84	18	38	46	6,699	33	2,810	14
II. Furniture	244	30,859	57	23	29	28	10,062	32	5,570	18
III. Footwear	102	25,709	40	39	19	21	10,854	42	330	1
IV. Cotton textiles	224	99,091	12	53	6	6	10,117	10	1,460	1
V. Hosiery	85	14,566	21	25	10	11	5,040	35	600	4
VI. Automotive parts	26	10,123	8	31	4	4	1,904	19	270	3
VII. Dresses	110	3,599	10	9	5	5	264	7	60	2
Totals[3]	1,251	203,960	232	16	111	121	38,251	19	11,100	5

1 The lower limits to plant size as measured by number of employees are as follows: industries II through V, inclusive, 21; industries I and VII, 8; industry VI, 50.

2 Only plants defined as comparable were studied. The differences between the employment in the plants studied and the number of workers whose rates were tabulated arise from the exclusion of incentive workers and from the fact that the rates of workers only in selected key occupations were tabulated by BLS.

3 The percentage figures shown in the row of totals are calculated from the data in that row, not from the figures in the percentage columns. All percentage figures have been rounded to the nearest whole per cent.

Source: Industry-Locality Studies, Bureau of Labor Statistics, Washington, D. C., 1950. Data in the form here analyzed have not been published.

summaries on forms OWR-23 by industry, city and occupation. Simultaneous breakdowns by industry, city, size of plant, unionization of plant, method of wage payment and occupation do not appear.

Typical of the reasons for excluding several industries from analysis are: the absence of nonunion plants, inexact specification of location, extreme product differentiation within industries and noncomparability of plant sizes.

The exclusion of workers paid an incentive rate raises two questions. First, how important numerically are incentive workers in the total employment in the plants studied? Second, how significant is the variation in the proportions of incentive workers as between union and nonunion plants? Since it is known that incentive workers generally have higher earnings than time workers, the requirements of internal rate structure alignment within plants might result in plants with a preponderance of these more highly paid workers paying higher rates to hourly workers. Consequently, for a comparison of wage rates in union and nonunion plants it is desirable that the proportions of incentive workers should not vary too widely.

For all 7 industries incentive workers constitute from 46.3 per cent of total employment in union plants to 51.7 per cent in nonunion plants, a difference of only 5.4 per cent. In paints and varnishes, however, less than 1 per cent of the work force is paid on an incentive basis while for footwear and dresses the figure is as high as 80 per cent. In only 6 instances do variations between proportions in union and nonunion plants differ by more than 10 per cent. The time workers studied thus comprise the majority of all workers and variations between union and nonunion plants are not large enough to affect the results of the study.

The analysis of the data was undertaken in the following manner: the plant was the unit of comparison. Within each industry and locality, union and nonunion plants of comparable size were selected. For each plant, the wage rate paid to time workers in each of several occupations was determined by striking a simple arithmetic average of the rates paid to all the time workers in the occupation. The occupational rate for union plants of given size is, again, a simple mean of the average paid in each plant. This mean is compared with the mean of rates paid for the same occupation in nonunion plants of this size.

In making wage-rate comparisons it was found possible to eliminate the effect of any sex differential that might exist. The fact is that, for the industries studied, given occupations are filled by either men or women but usually not by both. Most commonly, office employees are women, production workers are men. In textiles and dresses many production workers are women but the occupations they fill are generally not filled by men. In the few instances where both sexes were employed in an occupation, the occupation was divided into two groups, each containing one sex. Similarly, learners and apprentices were placed in a separate category and their rates in union plants were compared only with the rates of their counterparts in nonunion plants.

This method of measuring and comparing union and nonunion wage rates has eliminated the effect upon wage differentials of premium payments, geographic influences, variations in plant size and quality of work forces together with all dynamic elements. Since a fairly precise comparison of wage rates of comparable workers has been attained and since these workers are in sufficiently close proximity to allow for interplant mobility, it is proper to treat the differentials obtained as measures of the influence of unions upon wage rates.[7]

II. THE SIGNIFICANCE OF THE WAGE DIFFERENTIALS

Before presenting the results of the statistical analysis, an example may be given of the kind of wage comparisons that have been made. In Cleveland, Ohio, in April 1950 the following average wage rates were paid to maintenance men in the paints and varnishes industry: union plants, $1.470; nonunion plants, $1.500 (size of plants: less than 31 workers). Subtracting the nonunion rate from the union yields a differential of —$.030. A plus sign for the differential would thus have meant that, on the average, the union rate was higher. These differentials are the basic measures of the effects of unionism on wage rates. The problem of the present section is to assess the statistical significance of these differentials.

Chart 1 gives a graphic representation of the distributions of differentials by industry. Measuring the central tendency of each distribution by the mode shows that in five instances the typical differential lies in the class interval 0 to + 5 cents, suggesting a small positive advantage to union workers. In cotton textiles, however, the mode lies in the interval 0 to − 5 cents. Footwear, the only distribution not unimodal, is characterized by a central mode in this same negative interval.

A test of the significance of the number of differentials favoring union (or nonunion) workers may be developed on the assumption

[7] There are, of course, limitations to this mode of inquiry arising from the definition of the problem and from the nature of the statistical materials employed. Coverage of the data is relatively narrow for four industries: 600 workers in hosiery (21 plants in 5 cities), 270 workers in automotive parts (8 plants in 1 city), 60 workers in dresses (10 plants in 2 cities), and 330 in footwear (40 plants in 5 cities).

CHART I — DISTRIBUTIONS OF UNION, NONUNION WAGE RATE
DIFFERENTIALS BY INDUSTRY (in cents)

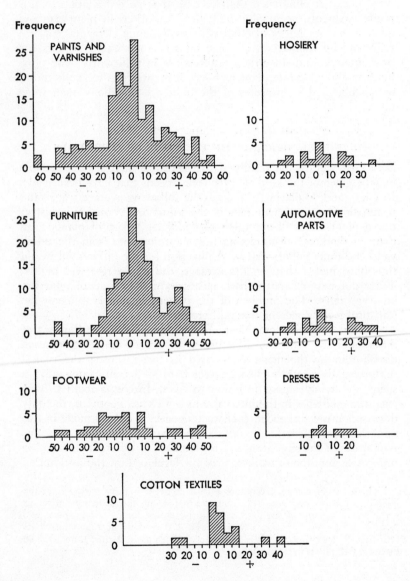

TABLE II — RESULTS OF SIGNIFICANCE TESTS OF THE NUMBER OF
DIFFERENTIALS FAVORING UNION WORKERS, BY INDUSTRY

Industry	Number of differentials		Probability
	Total	Positive	
I. Paints and varnishes	172	89	.7032
II. Furniture	126	87.5	.00006[1]
III. Footwear	39	12.5	.0246
IV. Cotton textiles	24	13.5	.5405
V. Hosiery	20	13	.2636
VI. Automotive parts	23	15.5	.0953
VII. Dresses	6	5	.2187
All industries	410	236	.0026

1 For probabilities of this small order, see H. Cramer, *Mathematical Methods of Statistics* (Princeton, 1946), p. 557.

that if the universe from which the differentials were drawn had contained equal numbers of positive and negative differentials and if our method of collecting data had been random, a sample would have been expected to yield, on the average, as many positive as negative differentials. It follows that the probability of getting various numbers of positive differentials is derived from the normal curve.

We may now ask, how significantly does the number of positive differentials obtained for all 7 industries taken together differ from the number to be expected from the hypothetical universe? For the 7 industries as a whole there are 410 rate comparisons, 233 of them positive. The probability of obtaining at least this number of positive differentials is .0026 or less than 3 chances in 1000. (Six instances of zero differentials have been equally divided between positive and negative.) This result is not consistent with the hypothesis that the universe contains as many positive as negative differentials. It appears that union rates are higher than nonunion rates in a significant number of instances.

For each of the 7 industries we may again ask how significant is the number of positive differentials. Table II presents the data and probability for each industry. If a level of significance of 1 per cent is adopted, there is one industry in which the number of positive differentials is significant, namely, furniture. The probability here is .00006. In footwear the probability is .0246, close to the significant level. From these results it may be tentatively concluded that in only 2 of the 7 industries is there a wage advantage. In furniture the advantage lies with workers in union plants; in footwear, a less clearly defined advantage lies with workers in nonunion plants.

Another summary measure, shown in Table III, is the mean differential for each industry together with the probability of obtaining such a value by random sampling from a universe in which the true mean is zero. At a 1 per cent level of significance, only for workers in the furniture industry are the results of these tests inconsistent with the hypothesis that the true mean is zero. In this industry the mean differential, $+ 7.57$ cents, is suggestive of union wage rates that are significantly higher than nonunion rates.

In only 3 of the 14 tests performed have the results shown differentials significant in number or magnitude. The hypothesis thus appears warranted that in most of the industries the observed wage differences may be normally distributed about a mean of zero and that departures from this distribution are attributable to errors in

TABLE III — RESULTS OF SIGNIFICANCE TESTS OF THE MEAN
DIFFERENTIAL BY INDUSTRY

Industry[1]	Mean in cents	Probability	t	t at 5%
I. Paints and varnishes	−.67	.7086		
II. Furniture	7.57	.00006		
III. Footwear	−3.72	.4459		
IV. Cotton textiles	1.83	.2616		
V. Hosiery	4.90		1.207	2.093
VI. Automotive parts	4.35		1.236	2.074
VII. Dresses	9.80		2.279	2.571

1 For industries V, VI and VII, the t test of significance has been used to compensate for the bias of small samples.

sampling. Unfortunately data are adequate for a test of this hypothesis only in the paints and varnishes industry. Here the value of X^2 is 30.32 while the values associated with 1 and 2 per cent levels of significance are 30.58 and 28.26, respectively. The normal curve is then a fair depiction of the actual distribution for this industry.[8]

Although the efficacy of unionism in causing rate differentials

8 Additional, but not independent, evidence in support of the contention that the sample distribution approaches closely the normal curve is found in the values of β_1 (measuring skewness) and β_2 (measuring kurtosis). For the normal curve these values are 0 and 3, respectively; in the present case the values are −.292 and 3.167 with associated probabilities of .109 and .645.

has been opened to serious doubt, it might be thought that in certain circumstances unionism might be more effective than in others. Thus, perhaps unions may be more effective in more highly paid occupations where there is greater specialization and greater inelasticity of demand for labor services. If this were so, a positive correlation would be expected between the average level of rates and the size of differential in various occupations.[9] Table IV shows the correlation be-

TABLE IV — CORRELATION OF THE LEVEL OF AVERAGE RATES AND THE SIZE OF DIFFERENTIAL IN OCCUPATIONS, BY INDUSTRY

Industry[1]	Correlation coefficient, R	Significant value of R	
		At 5%	At 1%
I. Paints and varnishes	.124	.632	
II. Furniture	.147	.553	
IV. Cotton textiles	−.389	−.632	
V. Hosiery	.015	.755	
VI. Automotive parts	−.685		−.641

1 Industries III and VII, Footwear and Dresses, are omitted because the number of paired variables, 2 in the former and 4 in the latter, is so small.

tween rate levels and differentials by industry. Except in automotive parts, there is no apparent relationship between the size of differential and the level of the average rate; coefficients range from − .389 in textiles to + .147 in furniture. At a 5 per cent level, these values do not differ significantly from zero.

A second relationship that might show the influence of unionism is that between the size of differential and the degree of unionization in the city area. As unionization progresses towards the inclusion of more plants, there is less competition from nonunion plants in both product and factor markets. This decrease in competition might permit unions to drive a more advantageous bargain with managements in the organized plants. To test this hypothesis, average differentials were computed for each city area within industries. These differentials were correlated with the percentages of unionized plants in these areas. Table V presents the results for the 3 industries for which sufficient data were available and for all industries taken together. As compared with the results from random sampling in a universe

[9] The possibility of a negative correlation must also be considered: unions may exert themselves chiefly in behalf of the less highly paid majority of members.

with zero correlation, none of the coefficients is significant at a level of 5 per cent: increased unionization of plants does not appear associated with increased wage differentials.

A final hypothesis is that the size of differential is related to the size of plant. It is known that in many industries, occupational wage levels vary positively with plant size.[10] A permissive factor that may in part explain this variation is economies of scale: larger plants may be able to carry further the specialization of some factors of production and to take advantage of other large, indivisible factors. It may be argued that large and small nonunion firms will pay the same competitive wage rate to the same kind of labor, while union firms may be compelled to pay higher rates in larger establishments. Thus the union-nonunion wage differential would be larger in larger plants. To test this hypothesis, average differentials have been computed for each size-of-plant category throughout the several city areas. These values have been correlated with the average plant size. For two in-

TABLE V — CORRELATION OF SIZE OF DIFFERENTIAL AND DEGREE OF
UNIONIZATION IN CITY AREAS, BY INDUSTRY

Industry[1]	Correlation coefficient, R	R at 5%
I. Paints and varnishes	−.065	−.602
II. Furniture	.339	.707
III. Footwear	.657	.811
All industries	.180	.339

[1] Cotton textiles (IV), Hosiery (V), Automotive parts (VI), and Dresses (VII) are omitted since data are available for only 3 cities in the first industry, 2 in the second and but 1 in the last 2. However, the coefficient for all industries includes these 4 industries.

dustries, cotton textiles and automotive parts, variance analysis has been used because of the small number of plant sizes in the few cities represented by the data. Table VI shows the correlation coefficients and the results of variance analysis. Neither of the values of z and only one of the 4 correlation coefficients is significant at a level of 5 per cent. In footwear only, the coefficient .676 is significant between levels of 1 and 2 per cent. The evidence does not support

[10] Verification of this observation is found in most of the *Wage Structure Bulletins of BLS*. For an authoritative discussion, see H. M. Douty, "Union, Nonunion Wages" in W. S. Woytinsky and Associates, *Employment and Wages in the United States* (New York, 1953), pp. 493–501.

the hypothesis that unionism is able to secure relatively higher rates for members in larger plants.

In 5 industries — paints and varnishes, cotton textiles, hosiery, automotive parts and dresses — there was found to be no significance to the number of average magnitude of union-nonunion wage-rate differentials. Nor could variation of the size of these differentials be

TABLE VI — RELATIONSHIP BETWEEN THE SIZE OF DIFFERENTIAL AND
THE SIZE OF PLANT IN CITY AREAS, BY INDUSTRY

Industry[1]		Correlation		
	Correlation coefficient, R	R at 5%	R at 2%	R at 1%
I. Paints and varnishes	.055	.381	—	—
II. Furniture	−.158	−.423	—	—
III. Footwear	.676	—	.658	.708
V. Hosiery	−.029	−.666	—	—
		Variance analysis		
	Size of plant	Variance	z	z at 5%
IV. Cotton textiles	under 500 500–1500	102.76 94.82	.0574	.5843
VI. Automotive parts	under 200 200–300 300–400	456.36[2] 315.03[3]	.3706	.6254

1 Dresses (VII) are excluded because there are only two size-of-plant groups, one containing 2 differentials, the other, 4.
2 Variation within size classes.
3 Variation among size classes.

explained with reference to wage structure (except, perhaps, in automotive parts), degree of unionization or size of plant. In these industries differentials are probably caused by a multitude of random forces; variation in observed magnitudes arises in this way and from errors in measurement. Unionism appears to be unimportant as a causal factor.

In footwear, nonunion workers appear to work at higher rates than union workers, judging by the number of differentials found to favor the former. The average magnitude of differential, however, while favoring nonunion workers, is not significant. Size of differential is not associated with the degree of unionization nor with the level of wage rates in occupations; size of plant may offer some explanation of the variation. Considering both the number and average magnitude of rate differentials, only in the furniture industry are workers in union plants employed at significantly higher rates than their nonunion counterparts. Other variables treated do not corroborate the evidence of the influence of unionism in this industry.

III. THE TIMING OF WAGE CHANGES AND THE CREATION OF DIFFERENTIALS

How can the dissimilar findings of significant wage differentials for the footwear and furniture industries be explained? Furthermore, how can these results be reconciled with those obtained in 5 other industries wherein no appreciable wage advantage either way is apparent?

A useful hypothesis for explaining these divergent results is that typically there are no significant differences in the wage rates of workers in union and nonunion plants. By typically is meant, during periods of wage stability throughout industry as a whole. This hypothesis, of course, rests largely upon the postulates of competitive equilibrium price theory. During periods of disequilibrium, of rapid wage change, however, union-nonunion rate differentials are likely to develop: there will often be leads and lags between wage movements in union and nonunion establishments. Hence, if a wage survey of some industry is conducted during a stable period, no significant differentials will be discovered, for it will require but a relatively short period of time, at most a few months, for wage rates of one group to catch up with those of the other. If the survey is conducted at a time of rapid change, differentials favoring either union or nonunion workers will appear.

It cannot be stated categorically whether rates of union workers will lead or lag the rates of nonunion workers. More frequently it is to be expected that nonunion firms will await the outcome of formal, widely publicized collective negotiations before instituting wage changes. However, anticipatory action cannot be precluded.

If an industry is highly organized, both nationally and on the particular local, city level for which wage data have been collected, it is likely that the minority of nonunion firms will feel constrained to conform to the wage patterns established through collective bargaining. Whether or not any patterns are in fact discernible will depend upon the scope of such bargaining. Where a few large companies and the unions with whom they deal negotiate master agreements covering most of the workers in the industry, nonunion firms will be under great pressure promptly to meet negotiated wage changes. But even if the industry is not highly organized nationally, this result will obtain when, on the particular local level, collective negotiations embrace a substantial portion of the industry. The existence of association-wide bargaining will enhance the forces acting upon the nonunion firm to adhere to negotiated wage changes.

Another factor that affects the creation of differentials is the relative inflexibility of contractually determined wage rates. If an inflationary situation develops during the life of a negotiated agreement that provides for no wage reopening, rates of unionized employees may remain unaltered. By contrast, the nonunion firm may quickly respond to such inflationary forces by raising wages. Needless to say, the attitude and strength respectively of labor and management must be considered along with the fact that the contractual rates usually hold for a stated time period.[11]

In order to bring the preceding discussion to bear on the explanation of wage developments in our 7 industries, we shall divide them into two groups: those for which wage data were collected in the relatively stable months of 1950, before the impact of Korean hostilities, and those surveyed thereafter. Chart 2 shows the behavior of average hourly earnings, excluding overtime, for all manufacturing and for each of the 7 industries during 1950.[12] From January to August, earnings in all manufacturing rose only 1.8 cents an hour or about a quarter of a cent per month; from August to December, however, the rise was 7.1 cents or over 1.7 cents per month. It will be seen that for the economy as a whole, the first seven or eight months of 1950 constitute a period of relative wage stability while the later months are characterized by rapid rises. Three of the five industries in which no significant differentials were found were surveyed in April, during the relatively stable period.

An examination of the individual earnings series for cotton textiles, paints and varnishes and automotive parts confirms this impres-

[11] Since contractually determined wage rates are generally held to be most inflexible in a downward direction, it is to be expected that wage differentials will develop more rapidly during periods of business recession. *Cf.* Douty, *op. cit.*, p. 499 and Slichter, *op.* cit., p. 333. The present analysis, however, is concerned with disparate wage movements in 1950, a year of wage stability in its first half and of rising wages thereafter.

[12] The use of average hourly earnings series on a monthly basis with overtime eliminated to determine the stability of wage rates or the timing of their change is not to be confused with their use as a measure of the magnitude of wage-rate changes.

sion of wage stability; none of the series shows an earnings change of as much as 3 cents an hour during the first 6 months of 1950.[13] Wage surveys in these industries show no significant wage differentials because of the absence of general wage movements that are prerequisites to the creation of such differentials. In the automotive industry, the dominance of a few large firms and of a single union provides additional reason for expecting pressures on nonunion firms that would cause them to meet promptly any negotiated wage changes.

While the dress industry was surveyed in August, the terminal month of the period of general stability, earnings here exhibit less than 3 cents change until and including the survey month. On a seasonally adjusted basis, earnings appear even more stable.[14] Again, confirmation of wage stability is found in *Current Wage Developments,* previously cited: during June, July and August, wage increases were reported for only 2,250 workers while in December the number had risen to 91,600. Here, too, the conclusion may be drawn that an absence of union-nonunion wage differentials was to have been expected in view of the prevailing wage stability. The dominance of union organization reinforces this conclusion.[15]

The hosiery industry, surveyed in October, displays a depression in its earnings series that may, in part, be attributable to seasonal variations in output and employment. Of more importance, however, are piece-rate revisions downward in April and upward in September, restoring rates to their earlier levels. Rates of time workers were not affected by either change. Not until January 1951 did a general rise in rates occur.

The furniture industry, which was found to have significant differentials favoring union workers, was surveyed in October in the midst of a steady rise in earnings: from August to December, aver-

---

[13] Detailed confirmation of wage stability is found in *Current Wage Developments,* Jan.-Aug. 1950, BLS, Nos. 25-32. See also the following BLS wage chronologies: *Chrysler Corp.,* 1948, No. 5; P. Arnow and J. W. Bloch, *General Motors Corp.,* 1951, No. 9; A. A. Belman, *Ford Motor Co.,* 1951, No. 14; and *Dan River Mills, Inc.,* 1943-1951 (unpublished).

[14] Seasonal adjustment is important in this industry which employs a large proportion of more highly-paid incentive workers. See W. S. Woytinsky, *Seasonal Variations in Employment in the United States,* Com. on Soc. Security, Soc. Sci. Research Council (Washington, 1939).

[15] The industry is between 80 and 100 per cent organized as measured by the proportion of workers covered by the terms of collective bargaining agreements. See *Extent of Collective Bargaining and Union Recognition,* Bull. No. 909, BLS, 1947.

CHART 2 — AVERAGE HOURLY EARNINGS, OVERTIME ELIMINATED, FOR
ALL MANUFACTURING AND FOR SEVEN INDUSTRIES IN 1950,
BY MONTH

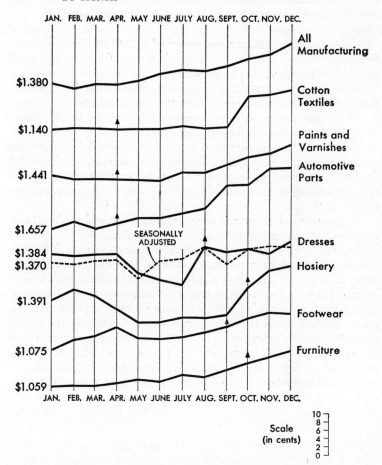

▲ Month in which wage survey was conducted in the industry

Source: *Handbook of Labor Statistics*, BLS, 1951, Table C-1. For the method of eliminating overtime see "Elimination of Overtime Payments from Gross Hourly Earnings,"
Mo. Lab. Rev., Nov. 1942, LV, 1053.

age hourly earnings rose 5.5 cents, an average monthly rise of slightly
less than 1.5 cents. Yet reported wage increases for union workers
are primarily confined to the months preceding October. Of some

60,000 union workers receiving wage increases, over 50,000 received them prior to the survey month. Thus, while data are unavailable to show that rates of union workers led those of nonunion, the inference may be suggested. The lack of a high degree of union organization supports this inference.[16]

The footwear industry was surveyed in September, in the middle of a continuous rise in earnings which began in July and terminated in November, and wage data show a significant number of differentials favoring nonunion workers. The reason for the better showing of nonunion workers is found in the fact that wage increases for union workers were largely confined to the month of October after the wage survey had been conducted.

The material considered so far has been broad in nature, not directly applicable to the selected group of workers to which our rate data in the present study pertain. In order to get a clearer picture of wage developments, a more detailed study of the footwear industry was made.[17]

The timing of changes in wage rates of unionized workers in the footwear industry in late 1950 is presented in Table VII. With minor exceptions, there appears to be considerable similarity in these wage movements, which is to be expected in view of the association-wide bargaining that characterizes the industry on the local, city level in most of New England. What might be called a pattern of increases is displayed, consisting of a 9 to 10 cent or 8 to 10 per cent rise in rates. Further, all of the increases in wages (excepting the restoration of an earlier wage cut in Auburn and Lewiston, Maine) came after the month of September when the Bureau of Labor Statistics conducted its survey of wage rates in footwear.

While negotiated rates were raised after September 1950, many nonunion firms granted wage increases much earlier although little or no publicity attended this action. In the Brockton area, where

---

[16] Information secured from labor and management sources in two of the cities represented in the present study agrees with these contentions. However, detailed data are scanty because of the multitude of very small firms and the absence of centralized collective negotiations.

[17] This discussion of the footwear industry is largely confined to those cities in New England for which data have been collected. In addition to trade publications the author consulted several authorities in the industry: G. P. Shultz, of Massachusetts Institute of Technology; J. Davis, of the New England Shoe and Leather Association; J. Mara, president of The International Boot and Shoe Workers Union (AFL); and J. F. Jankowski, president of the Brotherhood of Shoe and Allied Craftsmen (Ind.).

TABLE VII — NEGOTIATED WAGE INCREASES IN THE FOOTWEAR INDUSTRY
IN SELECTED NEW ENGLAND CITY AREAS, FALL 1950 AND
JANUARY 1951

Date of increase	City area	Number of workers affected	Hourly increase
Sept. 20, 1950	Auburn and Lewiston, Me.	1,800	7.5%[1]
Oct. 8	Worcester, Mass.	350	$.09[2]
Oct. 10	Brockton, Mass.	6,000	10%
Oct. 16	Worcester, Mass.	800	$.10
Nov. 15	Boston, Mass.	300	8%
Dec. 15	Auburn and Lewiston, Me.	3,000	8%
Jan. 2, 1951	Haverhill, Boston, Worcester, Mass.	15,000	$.10

[1] Restoration of a wage cut effected on Jan. 23, 1950.
[2] Piece-rate workers received an increase of $.07.
Source: *Current Wage Developments*, No. 33–37, BLS, Washington, Sept. 1950–Jan. 1951.

about 3,000 workers are employed in nonunion firms, wage increases of 6 cents an hour became effective during late July and early August. At this time negotiations were still in progress in the organized section of the industry. Other nonunion firms took similar initiative.

The 6-cent increase given by nonunion firms anticipated the outcome of collective bargaining negotiations that were going on in New England and in other areas of the country and thus constituted part of a pattern of wage change. This pattern culminated explicitly October 2 in the wage settlement between the International Shoe Company, the largest firm in the industry, and two unions, the United Shoe Workers of America (CIO) and the Boot and Shoe Workers Union (AFL). The contract applied to the wages and employment conditions of some 32,000 workers, although few of them were employed in the cities studied here. On the contrary, as negotiations were concluded in these cities during the last three months of 1950, a different pattern developed consisting of approximately either an 8 to 10 per cent or a 9 to 10 cent increase in rates. The wage differentials noted in footwear in September were thus created by the lead of nonunion rates ahead of union. When, at a later date, bargaining was concluded in the organized sector of the industry in New England, a different pattern emerged. Nonunion firms then generally met the larger increases that typified the industry in this part of the country, changing their earlier 6-cent raise to an increase equivalent to that gained by workers in unionized plants.

V. CONCLUSION

This study of union-nonunion wage rate differentials leads to the conclusion that, for the industries and occupations considered, there are no significant differentials between the rates of workers in union and nonunion plants; similar studies of a static nature have often revealed differentials which were most likely a function of variations in size of plant, method of wage payment, size of city, and other variables known frequently to be associated with both higher wage rates and greater unionization. In two instances where significant differentials were discovered, they were attributable to lags in the wage movements of one group of workers behind the other.

It follows from this that the results of surveys of wage rates of workers in union and nonunion plants must be cautiously interpreted with due regard for the economic context in which the data were collected. What might appear to be a wage advantage for one group may actually indicate a transient gap, quickly effaced by the passage of time.

To the extent that these findings are confirmed by more extensive research, the problem of this kind of wage-structure "distortion" caused by unionism can be set to one side. Investigations of the impact of unionism on wages may then assume a more aggregative character, attempting to discern union influences upon the structure of wages as among industries, geographic areas and eventually, if the model-builders' dreams are realized, upon the aggregate returns to different factors of production.

COMMENT

Although Maher found that the instances in which union wages were greater than nonunion levels were significantly more than half the cases for only one industry, he considered that for all the industries combined, that is, for all the comparisons made, union rates were higher in a significant number of cases. This finding seems to dilute the strength of the general theme throughout the article: that unions did not gain a long-run wage advantage for their members for the industries studied.

However, Maher concedes too much to the opposing view that union wages tend to be higher than non-union wages when he notes that 236 positive differentials statistically are significantly more than half the 410 total comparisons. He acknowledges that in furniture there are significantly more instances in which union levels are higher than nonunion than vice versa. Thus, to imply that there is a bias in favor of the union workers that is not strong enough to show statistical significance for the individual industries, but accumulates into a significant amount for all industries as a whole, requires elimination of the significant furniture industry in the calculations. Also eliminating the footwear industry, which is significant at the 5 per cent level in favor of the nonunion workers, there are only 136 out of the 255 remaining cases, or 53 per cent of this reduced total, in which union wages are higher than their nonunion counterparts. At the 5 per cent or even 1 per cent level, this ratio is not significantly greater than one-half the total adjusted number.

Thus, rather than conclude that, for the overall survey, union rates are higher than nonunion rates in a significant number of instances, Maher should have noted that this result was derived from the experience of one industry. A more meaningful conclusion would be that for furniture the difference was significant in favor of union workers and for footwear it was in favor of nonunion workers, but for the other industries, either individually or taken as a whole, there was no significant advantage either way, even though for all five of them there were more instances of union than nonunion wage advantage. (On this last observation, a statistician might wish to apply the concept of runs to test significance.)

It is interesting to note that Maher found no significant relationship between the size of differential and degree of unionization within the metropolitan areas in which the survey was made. (Maher isolated the variable, degree of local unionization, from his detailed study by limiting his comparisons to plants in the same area.) This finding suggests an important question which the nature of the data did not permit Maher to answer. Was there any relationship between degree of unionization within an industry and the size of the differential?

Maher's data only permitted a comparison of those plants for which over 50 per cent of the workers were covered by wage agreements with the other "nonunion" plants. Would significant differences have appeared between plants, say, 10 per cent organized compared with completely nonunion plants? Ross and Goldner, in a paper noted in the Reading Suggestions at the end of this volume, tried to study union influence by degree of unionization, but these conclusions were

somewhat indefinite on the effects of gradation of intensity of unionization.

Throughout, Maher focuses his research on the question of the
existence of a differential between union and nonunion wages. At
the very outset he announces that his study will not touch on the more
crucial but also more elusive issue of whether unions secure greater
wage gains for their members than they would have received had they
been unorganized, or the related more important question of whether
unions are a wage-increasing force. Although his formal analysis
does not refer to these latter questions, some of his observations and
conclusions do.

If his hypothesis that under stable conditions there will be no
significant difference between union and nonunion rates is valid, then
those who seek to find support for the view that unions do raise wages
by finding union-nonunion differentials are chasing a will-o'-the-wisp.
At the same time those who argue that market forces determine wages
will prove nothing by showing the absence of a differential, which may
be the result of "sympathetic pressure" instead of an indication of the
unimportance of union wage activity.

In Maher's presentation there is probably more support for the
power forces than the market forces school. He writes of leads and
lags in wage adjustments, which might merely represent the frictions
of adjustment to either power or market forces. However, in Maher's
analysis of these leads and lags, when the union wage changes lead
(furniture), nonunion wages respond in kind. When nonunion wages
rise first (footwear), it is in anticipation of a union wage increase.
Here we sense adumbrations of acceptance of the doctrine of sympathetic pressure. Friedman wryly notes that believers in sympathetic
pressure can never be wrong. It provides a "heads I win, tails you
lose argument" for the power forces school. "Periods when union
wages rose more than nonunion are pointed to as evidence that unions
raise union wages; periods when nonunion wages rose as much or
more than union wages, as evidence that unions raise nonunion
wages."

While it is true that if you rely on sympathetic pressure as an
explanation of parallel union-nonunion wage movements you can
never be proved wrong, this does not mean that you are never right.

We shall never "prove" whether unions raise wages; perhaps this is what makes the subject so intriguing.

SUMMARY

The papers included in this collection underline the uncertainty and indecision in assigning the major determinants of wage levels and wage movements. While Lester points out the weaknesses in the marginalist position, Machlup claims that the case against marginalism is not conclusive. While Dunlop presents statistical substantiation of the importance of marginal elements in wage movements, other detailed studies show instances in which marginal principles appear to play a minor role. While Ozanne can show that industrial wages were higher during unionized periods than in earlier nonunion years, Maher can present a cross-sectional study in which union wages are no higher than nonunion levels.

The reader should not infer that these writings were purposely selected to present a confused picture. The entire literature, a sample of which is presented in the Reading Suggestions which follow, contains many studies and arguments supporting both the market and power forces position without reaching a definite conclusion as to which set of forces dominates the wage-setting process.

All of the conflicting views and contradictory conclusions reached in these selections and in other works in the field should not lead the student to conclude that some writers use the right and others the wrong approach to the study of the issues, nor that some workers are more efficient than others in their handling of the methodological and statistical problems enumerated above. Rather he should realize that there is no single solution to the question of whether market or power forces are dominant in the determination of wages. The answer depends on the condition of the labor market under study; this is a difficult area for generalization.

SUGGESTIONS FOR READING

For general background to the controversy over marginal theory, any good Principles text will provide an exposition of the elements of the marginal productivity theory. The student might find Machlup's presentation, some of which has been omitted from this volume, a bit too abbreviated. A thorough but more advanced treatment is to be found in Allan Cartter, *Theory of Wages and Employment* (Homewood, Illinois, 1959). A simpler presentation is made by K. W. Rothschild, *The Theory of Wages* (Oxford, 1956). The more ambitious student might try sections of J. R. Hicks, *The Theory of Wages* (New York, 1932). These works do more than explain the theory, they point out its shortcomings as well. A comprehensive source for the problems involved in measuring productivity changes and refined measurements of productivity for industry groups is John W. Kendrick, *Productivity Trends in the United States,* National Bureau of Economic Research (Princeton, New Jersey, 1961). A similar study of productivity measurements at the firm level is found in John W. Kendrick and Daniel Creamer, *Measuring Company Productivity* (New York, 1961).

Related to points raised in the Lester-Machlup controversy on worker interest in non-pecuniary aspects of their jobs, Lloyd Reynolds and Joseph Shister found in their survey of a medium-sized New England manufacturing city, *Job Horizons* (New York, 1949), that wages were an unimportant element in job mobility. Charles A. Myers and W. Rupert Maclaurin, *The Movement of Factory Workers* (New York, 1943), reached the same conclusion from their study. Among works stressing the point that businessmen do not always strive to maximize profits are Melvin Reder, "A Reconsideration of the Marginal Productivity Theory," *Journal of Political Economy,* LV (October, 1947); R. A. Gordon, "Short-Period Price Determination in Theory and Practice," *American Economic Review,* XXXVIII (June, 1948); Lloyd Reynolds, "Wage Differences in Local Labor Markets," *American Economic Review,* XXXVI (June, 1946); and Reynolds, "Toward a Short Run Theory of Wages," *American Economic Review,* XXXVIII (June, 1948). In a study of utilities, Eli Clemens found that some adjustment to wage increases was by rate increases — marginal behavior — but that in some cases profits were allowed to fall — non-marginal behavior, "The Interdependence of Wage and Price Determination in the Regulated Industries," *American Economic Review,*

XLII, Papers and Proceedings (May, 1952). A discussion of the provisions of collective bargaining agreements that reduce the substitutability of capital for labor as an adjustment to wage increases can be found in Nathan Belfer and Gordon Bloom, "Unionism and the Marginal Productivity Theory," *Insights into Labor Issues,* ed. by R. A. Lester and Joseph Shister (New York, 1948). In another study, "Effectiveness of Factory Labor: South-North Comparisons," *Journal of Political Economy,* LIV (February, 1946), Lester found that firms in general considered their northern and southern labor to be of equal efficiency. This conclusion, if generalized, would indicate that regional wage differences could not be given the marginalist explanation of differences in labor efficiency.

For general background to statistical studies of the relationship between wage and productivity movements, Melvin Reder presents a thorough analysis of factors, including productivity, which lead to differential industrial wage movements in "Wage Differentials: Theory and Measurement," *Aspects of Labor Economics,* National Bureau of Economic Research (Princeton, 1962). For an advanced treatment of the wage-price-productivity interactions, see W. E. G. Salter, *Productivity and Technical Change* (Cambridge, 1960).

Related specifically to Dunlop's article, the Fabricant study which, as Dunlop noted, shows a low correlation between productivity and wage movements appears in Solomon Fabricant, *Employment in Manufacturing, 1899–1939* (National Bureau of Economic Research, Washington, D. C., 1942). Frederic Meyers and Roger Bowlby, "The Interindustry Wage Structure and Productivity," *Industrial and Labor Relations Review,* Vol. 7 (October, 1953) also found a low rank correlation between wage and physical productivity movements. Other statistical studies which generally showed little correlation between wages and productivity usually focused on the issue of union influence on wages. Clark Kerr treated the influence of price changes in the wage-productivity relationship in "The Short-Run Behavior of Physical Productivity and Average Hourly Earnings," *Review of Economics and Statistics,* XXXI (November, 1949). Two statistical studies which made use of the value concept and found a close relationship between value productivity and wage changes among industries are Sumner Slichter, "Notes in the Structure of Wages," *Review of Economics and Statistics* (February, 1950), and Richard Perlman, "Value Productivity and the Interindustry Wage Structure," *International Labor Review,* Vol. 10 (October, 1956). The interested student of theory will find an explanation of the conditions under which a low ratio of labor to total industry costs leads to an inelastic labor demand schedule in Lloyd Ulman, "Marshall and Friedman on Union Strength," *Review of Economics and Statistics,* XXXVIII (November, 1955).

In the article that follows Kerr's in *The Theory of Wage Determination,* Lloyd Reynolds also gives a summary of union influence on wage structure studies in "The Influence of Collective Bargaining on the Wage Structure in the United States." His conclusions differ somewhat from Kerr's. In fact, within one structure, the industrial, Reynolds considers the strength of unions in high-wage industries a widening force. (There is here an implicit acceptance of the view that unionism is an independent source of wage gains.) Another summary of studies of unions' influence on wage structure can be found in Lloyd Reynolds and Cynthia Taft, *The Evolution of Wage Structure* (New Haven, 1956). Dunlop's *Wage Determination under Trade Unions* (New York, 1950), is one of the earliest systematic theoretical and statistical studies of the elements involved in wage setting under collective bargaining.

With reference to Kerr's paper itself, being a summary of other studies, it provides the reader excellent bibliographical suggestions in its numerous footnote references. Ross' *Trade Union Wage Policy* and Dunlop's article in *The Theory of Wage Determination* present the concepts of unifying elements which lead to comparable wage demands among a group of workers and condition labor supply. Martin Segal, "Interrelationship of Wages under Joint Demand: The Case of the Fall River Textile Workers," *Quarterly Journal of Economics*, LXX (August, 1956), notes the strong pressures that exist among workers in the same economic environment to equalize wage gains, if not wage levels. He noted that employers recognized this pressure to the degree that they tended to pass on wage increases secured through collective bargaining to uncovered workers in the plant. Recent studies have found a strong tendency toward equalization of wage gains — in Dunlop's terminology, the presence of clearly defined wage contours — among groups of industries having common characteristics such as degree of unionization, extent of product concentration, and geographical location. In general these studies found that large unionized industries set the "key rate" and were the prime mover in the uniform pattern of wage changes that went along the entire wage contour. Ross found uniform wage movements in a group of strongly unionized heavy industries, "The External Wage Structure," *New Concepts in Wage Determination*, ed. by George Taylor and Frank Pierson (New York, 1957). John Maher, "The Wage Pattern in the United States, 1946–1957," *International Labor Review*, Vol. 15 (October, 1961), emphasized the role of the key bargainer whose similar wage changes are diffused in varying strength throughout the industrial economy. For a similar view see Otto Eckstein and Thomas A. Wilson, "The Determination of Money Wages in American Industry," *Quarterly Journal of Economics*, LXXVI (August, 1962).

For general background on union influence on interindustry wage structure, three widely studied works are Joseph Garbarino, "A Theory of Interindustry Wage Structure Variation," *Quarterly Journal of Economics*, LXIV (May, 1950), Arthur Ross and William Goldner, "Forces Affecting the Interindustry Wage Structure," *Quarterly Journal of Economics*, LXIV (May, 1950), and Harold Levinson, *Unionism, Wage Trends and Income Distribution, 1914–1947* (Ann Arbor, 1951). None of these sources found unionism a particularly strong influence on wage

movements. Garbarino attributed greater weight to productivity and industry concentration than to unionism, and Ross and Goldner, just as Paul Douglas had found in his *Real Wages in the United States, 1890–1926* (Boston, 1930), concluded that only new unionism was a source of wage advantage. Levinson found unions influential only in keeping wages up during depressions, but he coined the expression "sympathetic pressure" by way of suggesting that parallel wage movement of union and non-union workers could possibly be explained by the extension of union wage pressure into the non-union sector. H. Gregg Lewis, "The Effects of Unions on Industrial Wage Differentials," *Aspects of Labor Economics,* presents a statistical analysis of studies of union influence on industrial wages. He finds unionism of varying, but generally minor importance as a wage-increasing element. Dunlop comments briefly on Lewis' conclusions immediately following.

With reference to Ozanne's paper, George P. Schultz and Charles A. Myers, "Union Wage Decisions and Employment," *American Economic Review,* XL (June, 1950), find that unions are employment-conscious during recessions. One of the reasons that Ross offered for union lack of interest in employment effects of wage demands is the availability to employers of adjustments other than employment reduction as a response to wage increases. Kirk Petshek, "The Tie between Wages and Employment," *Industrial and Labor Relations Review,* Vol. 4 (October, 1950), points out that the reasons suggested by Ross — increased efficiency and improved technology — are themselves labor saving. Two studies of the hosiery industry show that during bad times union leadership is generally more employment-conscious than the rank and file membership — George W. Taylor, "Hosiery," *How Collective Bargaining Works* (New York, 1945), and Joseph Shister, "The Theory of Union Wage Rigidity," *Quarterly Journal of Economics,* LVII (August, 1943). For a criticism of Ozanne's use of average income per worker instead of the distributive shares method in measuring union influence on wages, see Lowell E. Gallaway, "Impact of Unions on Wage Levels and Income Distribution: Comment," *Quarterly Journal of Economics,* LXXIV (May, 1960). Ozanne's defense of his procedure follows this *Comment* in his *Reply.* Spokesmen for Ozanne's view that unions are a source of wage increases are Charles Lindblom, *Unions and Capitalism* (New Haven, 1949), and Henry Simons, *Economic Policy for a Free Society* (Chicago, 1948). A frequently cited view that unions have little effect on wages is Milton Friedman, "Some Comments on the Significance of Labor Unions for Economic Policy," *The Impact of the Union,* ed. by David McCord Wright (New York, 1951).

Referring to the *Comment* on Maher's paper, Friedman's remarks on sympathetic pressure appear in his "Comment on Ulman's 'Marshall and Friedman on Union Strength,'" *Review of Economics and Statistics,* XXXVII (November, 1955). It should not be thought that Maher's findings of no significant difference between union and non-union wages

is the general result of statistical studies on this question. Harry M. Douty, "Union and Nonunion Wages," *Employment and Wages in the United States,* W. S. Woytinsky and Associates (New York, 1953), found union wages to be higher than non-union wages in 31 of 32 industries. Two detailed industry studies which showed a differential in favor of the union workers are Joseph Scherer, "The Union Impact on Wages: The Case of the Year-Round Hotel Industry," *International and Labor Relations Review,* Vol. 9 (January, 1956), and Stephen Sobotka, "Union Influence on Wages: The Construction Industry," *Journal of Political Economy,* LXI (April, 1953). However, on a broader level, Walter A. Morton concluded that in the immediate post-World War II period, union wage demands were made in response to the market force of price increases; his implication is that unionism itself was not then an independent wage-increasing element, "Trade Unionism, Full Employment and Inflation," *American Economic Review,* XL (March, 1950). For the view that unions are actually a stabilizing force in inflationary periods in that union wages are set for specified contract periods and are not subject to short-run pressures, a view somewhat supported by Maher's findings, see Kenneth Boulding, "Collective Bargaining and Fiscal Policy," *American Economic Review,* XL, Papers and Proceedings (May, 1950).